SURROUNDED BY
IDIOTS

Drop the Distractions,
Embrace Your Purpose
and
Get Your Ass in Gear

TONY DUFRESNE, PHD

Published by:
Java Bud

ISBN: 978-0-692-98928-9

Cover and interior design: Gary A. Rosenberg
www.thebookcouple.com

Printed in the United States of America

To the one who truly deserves it
more than anyone else—*you.*

*Thank you for entrusting your hard-earned money
and time to me. I know how hard it is to confront
change and challenge yourself to learn and grow.
You've got balls, and your commitment to make
your life something extraordinary will pay off.*

Contents

■ STEP 2: YOU'VE GOT TO OWN IT

■ STEP 3: TIME TO LIVE IT

Introduction to the Awe-Inspiring Multimedia Experience That Awaits You

FROM THE VERY BEGINNING OF THIS PROJECT, I wanted to create something you would be able to learn from and have some fun with on multiple layers. And, since one of my favorite approaches to teaching is making videos to go along with the concepts I talk about, I thought it would be a cool idea to insert some video links throughout this book to supplement the learning process. Truth be told, most of the videos I made for this book are more for your comedic enjoyment with a little learning stuff thrown in just to keep us honest in our journey to world domination.

So, as you go through this book, you will see a box that indicates where I've inserted a video. Just go to my website, **javabud.com**, click on the "Book Videos" tab, and then add in your email address. I'll immediately send you an email with all of the video links. So, if you're reading along and you come across "Video Time: Video #1," then just click on the Video #1 link in the email and you will immediately be transported into the amazing world of the multimedia experience.

I would now like to direct your attention to the first video, which happens to be a little "Welcome" message from me.

 **VIDEO TIME: VIDEO #1**

Do People Annoy You?

AFTER YEARS OF PAINSTAKING RESEARCH (which I like to refer to as life), I have come to this conclusion—nay, the realization that . . .

People Annoy Me.

But my impatience for the idiots who seem to surround me everywhere I turn (hello, Costco on a Saturday) actually has nothing to do with them; people annoying me has everything to do with me. My ability to generalize the entire population as annoying stems directly from the expectations I have for myself.

So, I'm going to take a big leap here and assume that you picked up this book because on some level you too are annoyed by people and/or by how things operate around you. In short, you look around yourself in undeniable amazement and come to the conclusion the idiots are taking over the world.

If this is so, I say to you:

Welcome, my friend, to the show that never ends.

The shitty news is there's a strong possibility that people will always annoy you. But the good news is, there is a reason why you feel like you're surrounded, and understanding what fuels this deep annoyance is the key to beating those fools at their own game. Because, as hard as it might be to believe, you are actually more frustrated with yourself than you are with the people around you.

It's like suddenly you've turned into Jim Carrey's character from *The Truman Show,* a movie about an orphan whose life is filmed as a television show without his knowledge until he discovers the truth and decides to escape. In the final scene, Truman tries to flee on a sailboat headed off into the horizon. But instead of his boat sailing off into the great blue, he hits a blue wall, a cement horizon enclosing the set that was the only world Truman had ever known.

Now, you look around at who is running things, what notoriety looks like, how fame is determined, what "trumps" talent these days, and who dates or marries whom, and being annoyed becomes an understatement. That is because you are Truman, who has banged against the wall of your current understanding of how the world works to receive a dose of reality: It doesn't have to be your world, and you have a choice. And, even though you don't yet know what lies beyond that great blue wall or how to get to the other side, at least you have the realization that there is, in fact, something more out there for you—the life you know you want to live.

It was my frustration with the feeling of being trapped in a world full of idiots that led me to search for more, to stop wondering if "this was as good as it gets," and to look past the wall I was constantly bumping up against (which explains my flattened skull ridge and diminished brainpan).

My experience on this journey to live a more fulfilling life has led me to share the stuff I've figured out along the way so that you won't talk yourself out of the life journey that you know you *must* take.

You have already reached that level of awareness where you know your life doesn't seem right, like there's something off. You may not know the exact reason, but you just know something ain't kosher. It's like you're squeezing into a pair of old underwear that you know is too small, but you'd rather live with the distorted fact that you can still wear them even though your waist is bulging out like a roast with a string tied around it.

Surrounded by Card-ashians

So, you've reached a level of understanding that life around you isn't really "flowing" like it should, which leads to frustration, which leads to being annoyed by the people around you, which leads to you feeling like you're surrounded by idiots.

Now, for the record, there are a lot of card-carrying idiots out there. My infantile brain just thought of an idea: call them Card-ashians. Taking these meatballs out of the equation, you're still going to find that even some of your *favorite* people will be insanely annoying to you at certain times of your life.

Actually, or I should say ironically, I'm sure you have realized that sometimes it's the person or people closest to you that are the most annoying when you are going through a Personal Frustration Level-9 Crisis Meltdown. This is, for the lack of a better term, normal and expected because these are the people you feel most comfortable displacing your shit on because the frustration is . . .

Wait for it . . .

Disappointment in yourself for being in an unfulfilling life bubble. It's being pissed at yourself for continuing to, apparently, make the wrong choice, getting yourself deeper in your shit, and *not* having any immediate answers to fix the things in your life that aren't working.

Again, I say, WELCOME!

Because, first and foremost, there isn't a person who has walked the earth who hasn't dealt with the gruesome aftermath of a bad decision and found themselves without a clue as to how to get themselves out of that hole. The good news for you is, all this crap is really a sign of growth and a sign that you are ready to take it to the next level, to open yourself up to the limitless possibilities that lie on the other side of that wall you keep slamming into. And that's where I come in.

Why Should You Read This Book?

For the sake of being totally transparent, I have never been a fan of the "introduction" section of a book. For some reason, I always thought that if the stuff in the intro was relevant, then why wasn't it Chapter 1? I mean, what's the point of an introduction? So, nine times out of eight, I would fake-speed-read with the spaz index finger swiping my way through the introduction, so I could quickly get to the meat and potatoes of the book. Which leads me to being directly confronted with the question of including an introduction in this book. And, what do you know, I finally get it!

In choosing to write my own introduction and in the process of doing so, I realized that this section is HUGE in explaining to you the benefits you will get from giving your valuable time to reading this book. Come to find out, the introduction is just that: an introduction of myself to you. It's like . . . the first Tinder pic, the Match profile, or the "Hey, how you doin'?" boxer-brief-in-a-dirty-bathroom-mirror-selfie-Twitter-dick pic.

This is my "*Shark Tank* Pitch" without the excessive flop sweat. Because, for you to get the most out of this book, I must effectively communicate to you:

◆ Who the hell I am

◆ Why I wrote this book

◆ Why you should read this book

◆ What you will get from this book

◆ What outcome you can expect from reading this book

Hello, My Name Is . . .

I've always wanted to start out a story by saying, "I was born a poor black child," which nowadays would probably be considered borderline racist, and the joke usually doesn't land because the movie reference is so old, being from the 1979 comedy classic *The Jerk*. But that is me, and a small sampling of the weird shit that swirls around my mind 24/7.

The reason I'm sharing this part of me with you is because, shockingly, this type of fringe reality that exists in my head didn't exactly mesh well with my family or my life experience as a kid.

I grew up in a home with parents who did everything they could to give my sisters and me a good life but ultimately ran the house and our lives based on fear—fear of not having enough money, fear of making waves, fear of conflict, fear of the neighbors' judgment, fear of self-expression that would lead to any extra attention toward me and, God forbid, the family, and a crushing fear of failure . . . or success (both fears actually come from the same place, which we'll talk about later).

I never bought in to the overimportance my parents gave money, to measuring self-worth with dollars. But still, I couldn't escape the conflict it created inside me, leading me to overvalue the importance of money as *the* measure of worth, instead of what I knew deep down, which was to be true to myself and figure out how I defined and valued my life and how I could discover and share my unique gifts with the world. The bottom line is, the forced belief that the accumulation of money would fulfill me really fucked me up. So it's probably no surprise to you that, try as I might, sometimes my strange inner reality would hit its head up against the wall of the family's conformity bubble. This usually ended up in a general lack of support whenever I wanted to try new things or tried to express myself in a way that might bring me and my family added attention.

And when I got a chance to really stretch my wings, usually there was so much fear of judgment or it was so "out of the box" that my parents would only be able to muster up lukewarm levels of validation and/or support at best, all the while hoping that my "crazy" or "imbalanced" phase would pass and I would come back to the flock.

Looking back, I completely understand that my parents' lack of support in those instances was a "them" thing and had nothing to do with validating me and my True Self and my worth, but, you know, as kids, we look to our parents to support our blossoming individuality. And, if you, as a kid, decided to throw your balls over the fence and let your inner crazy out, and there's no parental net to catch you and wrap you up and make you feel validated in your expression, then you tend to question yourself and your dreams. And on those occasions when I felt that burning need to just be my weird self, there was no real net to speak of, which, over the years, led to less and less authentic outbursts and more and more internal strife because that energy has to go somewhere. So, hello migraines and stress eating and debilitating self-judgment and almost zero self-worth. All my authentic energy that I preferred to put to use by singing badly and dancing in the produce section of the supermarket I now contained tightly inside me.

My resistance to my True Self led me to become very bitter, always on the defensive with people, hypersensitive to what others would say to me and about me, jealous of people around me who had the courage to accept and live as their authentic selves, and envious of the people who had an aura of self-assuredness about them. You know these people, the ones who just seem to naturally attract good things.

I still remember one instance, very specifically at a very young age, when I was talking with my childhood friends Janet and Jim, and I mentioned that I "pretty much hate everybody" (not them, of course). And, without hesitation, Janet replied, "That's really sad." I remember just brushing off her comment with a smug shoulder shrug, but of course, I knew she was right, and that made me feel even shittier about myself. The downward spiral continued.

I managed to survive the high school years, doing pretty well with grades and making some friends and playing some sports, all the while feeling the pressure of the inner volcano building from all the stuff I already talked about—conformity and fear—which ultimately took the form of a massive perfectionist identity.

Then, it was off to college where I was going to be an engineer. Why an engineer? Uh, oh yeah, because I was good at math and my parents said that would be a steady, well-paying job. Needless to say, my undergrad career was brutal, even for a kid who graduated near the top of his high school class and with a marginal level of common sense. Nonetheless, it was all difficult because I was on the *wrong path*. I was on my parents' path, which was the engineer and steady job and two-week vacation and PTO . . . *Ahhhhh!* What an effin' nightmare!

By some miracle (seriously, I don't know how I did it), I graduated and found myself in a real estate–appraising job that, even though it wasn't engineering (that dream lasted only three weeks), still wasn't the job for me, but it paid well, so I slipped into it like an old man into a warm bath, my Life Alert necklace within panic-grab distance.

Cold-Cocked, Compliments of the Universe

And then it finally happened—the point where it all changed!

I wanted to start working with a buddy of mine in a commercial brokerage firm, and the one requirement was to attend this business seminar, which was actually *not* a business seminar but a self-improvement type of seminar. He knew telling me it was a business thing would be the only way he could get me to go, and he was right.

So, I'm sitting in the audience and the facilitator starts talking about personal relationships and fears and failure and intimacy stuff, and I'm like, *WTF, man? Am I in the wrong room? Where's the PowerPoint presentation on*

"How to Bore the Hell Out of Your Clients with a Pointless PowerPoint Presentation"?

I was pissed, confused, a little scared, and . . . uh oh . . . here come the meat sweats! And because I'm an idiot and got there a little late and couldn't find an end-of-the-row seat in the back of the room for a possible quick and discreet exit if needed (usually my go-to move), I found myself mid–front row, flanked by two hygienically liberal strangers, so I decided to pretty much lean into it and see what happened.

There's Always Good News and Bad News

Now, like anything, there is a good and bad component to an experience like this. The seminar finally empowered me to be real with myself, to open up the channel and let my True Self exist. But in order to do that, the foundation of my reality at that time, which was based on all the crap I talked about, like the money-worth thing and fear of acceptance and people pleasing, etc., was completely blown to smithereens, resulting in a complete freefall.

Have you ever had the dream that you were falling and you kept reaching out to see if you could grab onto anything before you became a stain on the canyon floor, *à la* Wile E. Coyote?

That's how I felt. And as much as I needed to purge that shitty persona I constructed over the years, blowing it up with one atomic bomb was a bad idea. In admitting that I hated my job and I wasn't happy with most of my relationships and I'd wasted so much time living my life based on others' expectations, I collapsed into a deep depression, like a borderline nervous breakdown. Everything in my life was a sham, a mockery—a *shamockery*. What had I done?

And, in the process, I lost my job, my house, all my toys (motorcycle, jet ski, boat, yada, yada, yada), all the stuff I had previously used to validate my worth. This, my friend, was textbook self-sabotage. I found myself moving in with my grandparents, $70,000 in debt, starting all over again, with no idea what I was going to do.

Why the Atomic Bomb Approach Is So Bad for You

One of the main reasons I wrote this book was to keep you from setting off the atom bomb when you discover you're not where you want to be and you want to make some serious changes in your life. Over the years, I've found that there's a much better way to make your transition to a more authentic life than to completely obliterate everything.

You have got to untie your knots one at a time. I'll talk about this better approach later in the book.

For the record, I hesitantly went back to the appraising job, reframing it as a necessary tool to continue to function in the world (you know, buy food and pay rent), as I got a foothold on my path to figuring out why I'm here and what I have to offer as a coach and mentor.

So, that brings me back to you, and why I wrote this book for you.

I want this book to be a tool you can use over and over to familiarize yourself with the concepts so you can reground and refocus yourself as you take your steps toward expanding your life. My goal is to get you to a point where you know the inner workings of "you" and the hidden rules of the world so well that you don't even have to think about any tools or tricks or methods or theories. I want you to get to the point where you own them. It's like tying your shoes; you can do it quickly and efficiently without even having to think about what you're doing.

This book will be a part of creating a system that guides and supports your expansion into a seemingly effortless, consistent, deeply fulfilling, and purposeful meaning.

Your Plan to Immediate Results

I've tried to simplify it by narrowing my whole life theory formula down to $3\frac{1}{2}$ steps. (I included the $\frac{1}{2}$ part to be something different when people look at the title. Just being honest.) That being said, the $\frac{1}{2}$ step is legit and basically sets the tone for the three steps that follow. And, since I fashioned this book after the program manual I give all of my "I want more out of my life" clients who work with me, the steps are set up to build upon each other, leading to . . . wait for it . . .

An Action Step

Ha! Did you feel that shiver just shoot down your spine?

To put it bluntly, your time of reading self-help books and getting fired up and then not knowing where to go with all that energy and then seeing that energy piss itself away in indecision about how to use it, well . . .

THAT STOPS RIGHT THE FUCK NOW!

Together, you and I will baby-step ourselves through this book of learning and awareness and decision-making. And then, with your new, fresh, focused, guided energy, I will assist you in thinking, planning, and doing a small, but impactful project that will benefit you and at least one other person.

Honestly, that is the goal I have for you in writing this book and the reason why this book will actually produce measurable results for you. I guarantee, by the time you finish this book and complete an action step, your focus will shift from the annoying idiocy that surrounds you to your own empowered life possibilities. In a nutshell, you will still be surrounded by idiots, but it won't affect you anymore. Your focus will be square on yourself and creating the life of your choosing.

This Is How It's Going to Work

The first $\frac{1}{2}$ step of the plan is basically an argument for doing something totally batshit crazy, along with a guarantee of what this book can do for you.

Step 1 is all about knowledge. I will share my theory of how the world around you actually functions and how you can better understand it and ultimately make it your bitch with some sweet tools and techniques.

In **Step 2**, you will take an honest look at your current life and compare it to how it could be. Then you will be able to figure out what you need to do to get from here to there.

Then, in **Step 3**: ACTION, JACKSON! Nothing, and I mean *nothing*, will *ever* change if you don't take action. This is where you take all the fun stuff you've learned during our time together and put it into a small project that you create in order to prove to yourself that you can start and finish something that fires you up and, more important, is an asset to at least one other person out there besides yourself.

Seriously, this is the part that no one will ever be able to do for you. You can read a thousand self-help books and go to a hundred seminars and get super-duper knowledgeable about how the world works and where you're at and what you need to do to create the life you want to live, but it will never happen unless you put the potato bong down, brush the nacho cheese dust off your shirt, put on some pants, and make it happen.

I know I can't come to your house and stick my hand up your ass and move you around like a puppet. There are two things very wrong with that scenario, the first one being the most obvious: I don't know your address. The second is, it's not my job; it's yours and yours alone. That being said, I will be with you and fully supportive of you.

Baby Steps to the Door . . . Baby Steps to the Elevator

I've structured this book in a way that you will be able to use at least a couple of the tools and techniques I talk about to take immediate action. (I give you a bunch—just pick one or two that make the most sense to you or seem to be a natural choice that doesn't put you into a panic when seeing yourself using it.) And, as you will find out, my secret formula is pretty simple; it's about taking small, baby steps.

Remember my story about me completely blowing myself up and ending up in a freefall? Well, that's why I'm a big fan of small steps and that's why I know I've set this book up to lead you to where you need to be. I'm practically going to move your limbs for you as you read this book. Again—and I can't stress this enough—action is the most important step, and the only way to make anything stick is if you take small steps.

Seriously, Relax!

MY INTRODUCTION, WHICH I ONCE THOUGHT would be meaningless, has come to an end, and now it's time to jump in and make some shit happen. So, I leave you with this:

The ENTIRE point of this book is to take the pressure off, to free you of the mind-set that it's too late to have the life you've always wanted or that:

♦ The life you want is out of reach for some reason

♦ You're not worth it

♦ You don't deserve it because you've done some shady shit in your day

♦ You're too clueless to ever figure out the "meaning" of your life (which actually evolves through every thought, decision, and action you take every day) and live your life with a level of joy and fulfillment that you never knew you could keep around longer than a good orgasm or a free meal (they just taste better when they're free, and the meal's not such a bad deal either)

You are surrounded by idiots because . . .
you are also an idiot,
but so am I.

We all are, or could be, when we are not dialed into what's important to us.

 **VIDEO TIME: VIDEO #2**

The First ½ Step

CHAPTER 1

The Power of
a Restaurant Serenade

"You should bring something into the world that wasn't in the world before. It doesn't matter what that is. It doesn't matter if it's a table or a film or gardening—everyone should create. You should do something, then sit back and say 'I did that.'"

—RICKY GERVAIS

REMEMBER THAT SEMINAR I MENTIONED EARLIER? Well, I got so much out of that one that I signed up for the "next level" course, which involved mining down deeper into the chasms of my being to get an even better handle on who I was and what my life was all about. And, being relatively new at the whole self-improvement thing, I had no idea the levels of pain and discovery and horror and purposeful challenges that awaited me. One such daunting challenge was forced upon me by the group facilitator just before our lunch break on the second day of the five-day seminar.

As much as I thought I was a real team player in sharing with the group during the first day and halfway through the second, Jeannie, the facilitator, thought otherwise.

And as much as I attempted to explain my demeanor as a really good "active listener" or "mysteriously enigmatic," she saw right through it and called "bullshit," leading her to the conclusion that I was taking the easy way out by not opening up and being more vulnerable by sharing my deep, dark secrets. So, for my blatant insubordination, she decided to wield her proverbial Hammer of Thor at me in the following manner...

I don't remember her exact words, but it went a little something like, "When we go to lunch, you will stand up in the middle of the restaurant and sing a song."

"Okay. Wait . . . what?!"

Next thing I knew, I found myself sheepishly leaning up against the crouton-heavy salad bar station in the middle of a Marie Callender's restaurant.

Like a terrified kid on the high dive board, knowing his fate of merciless never-ending ridicule if he even thinks about coming back down the ladder, I focused on a patch of worn mauve wallpaper, with translucent red vertical stripes and rose stems, drew in a relative deep and somewhat shaky breath, and began to sing, "Chestnuts roasting on an open fire, Jack Frost nipping at your nose . . ."

For the record, it was a couple of weeks before Christmas, and, to be honest, I suck at remembering song lyrics unless they've been subconsciously burned into my brain over decades of passive listening, so I went with a classic.

As my impromptu a cappella performance began in earnest, my seminar group (including Jeannie, the facilitator) were huddled together in a separate banquet room, which was located behind me and out of view. Basically, they were nowhere in sight, but within earshot of every note of my impromptu performance.

Unable to face the potentially mortified faces of my unwilling audience, I turned the corner on the first verse with my serenade—"Tiny tots, with their eyes all aglow, will find it hard to sleep tonight . . ."—all the while burning a hole with my intense gaze into the faded but soothing wallpaper patch sitting about halfway up the back wall.

I'm thinking, *So far, so good*, at this point.

I quickly took a running inventory of my progress. I've been avoiding eye contact, maintained decent pitch, and my pace appeared to be good. And then, *Uh oh, we may have a situation here!*

My overly critical peripheral vision spotted two guys who both got their hair cut at Rico's Butter Knife and Bowl Salon and Spa, sitting directly in front of me showing the first signs of "the uncomfortable squirm." You know the one, where you simultaneously shift your cargo to the other butt cheek while mumbling your growing astonishment to your buddy, focused intently on *not* making eye contact with the "probably homeless" dude belting out a holiday tune while you're just trying to fit a quick soup and salad in before returning to your dispensary job?

This is too much "real" for them! I better speed up the pace a bit and fade out gracefully after the second verse. "Merry Christmaaaaas, toooooo youuuuuuuuu!"

I immediately fell into an adrenaline-fueled sense of, *Holy crap, I did it!*

And just as I ended my internal high-fives for surviving said stunt, my focus swiftly pivoted to my surrounding environment, which, if you recall, consisted of a restaurant during the lunch rush, with people eating their lunch in a restaurant. And, at that very second, I realized I was enveloped in a thick blanket of complete and absolute, hear-a-pin-drop silence.

I'd just inexcusably interrupted the usual normal dining experience for an entire restaurant and no one appeared to have the means to immediately process what I just did, including myself!

I was standing there like an idiot, feeling completely exposed and vulnerable, like that naked dream, a little liberating, yet horrifying at the same time.

Time had officially stopped, and, seriously, it seemed like a good thirty excruciating seconds ticked before the inescapable silence was broken with the most visceral collective bellowing of hoots and cheers I had ever heard.

It was my big group in the separate banquet room!

Since they were "in on the joke," so to speak, they were able to more quickly return to their senses. Damn it if that wasn't the sweetest sound I had ever heard in my life!

It was like a virtual auditory floating doughnut thrown from the Fiesta Deck of a passing Mexican party cruise ship to one very grateful guy on the verge of drowning in his own mortification.

Then, a Festivus Miracle!

My unsuspecting dining-room audience of strangers just trying to have a decent lunch began to regain their foothold and fell into rank and started clapping and cheering as well.

The collective validation for my what-the-hell-is-he-doing? caper snapped *me* back to reality just enough to acknowledge the grateful grazing hoards with a sweeping hand gesture of gratitude.

And, as I turned to make my way up the relatively wide two-step incline back to my own peeps in the secluded banquet room, I noticed the entire restaurant staff returning to their posts after being pulled away from their grill and washing duties to witness my potential train wreck.

As I entered the back banquet room, all I could see was a sea of people loud-clapping, you know, the fired-up clap with the hands raised high above the head. And then, a consistent barrage of back slaps followed, leaving me honorably massaged in the process.

The look of fascination on my group's collective grills was one part amazement that someone would actually pull off a stunt like that and another part amazed that I'd *nailed* it.

Now, at this point, I have to let you in on a little secret: What no one in the group knew was that I had actually been a lead singer in a band for a handful of years prior to this serenade. And, interestingly enough, Ms. Jeannie Facilitator challenged me to "sing a song in the middle of the restaurant" because she thought I was being a bit of a non-sharing, somewhat mysterious d-bag who needed a way to endear myself to the group.

At this point, I made my way to my seat, slightly out of breath, head still spinning. As I picked up the menu to peruse the lunch specials, our server entered the room and introduced herself, looked straight at me from across the long conference-sized dining table, and said, "That was great! We really enjoyed your song, but there's a problem."

Oh shit! I thought, *I offended some anti-Christmas diners, and they're complaining to the manager.*

She continued, "It seems the people in the bar area couldn't hear you that well and want you sing again for them."

Still slightly buzzed from the original event and along with the knowledge that this time it was expected and actually requested, I pushed my seat back and followed the server to the bar where I sidled up against the beverage service station and, for the second time, sang "The Christmas Song."

While I didn't get as big of a charge from the second time, the people in the bar seemed to enjoy it, and, in the process, I apparently impressed the server, who wound up asking me out on a date!

The Moral of the Story

So, there you have it, all true, happening to me while I was attending a personal development seminar a number of years ago. Coincidentally, the subject we were tackling before leaving for lunch break was, "Why are we so scared to be ourselves?"

In throwing myself out there that day, I finally felt again what it was like to just be "me" and to own my life fully and in that moment. I didn't just survive the moment—I'd never felt more alive!

So, of course, that brings me back to you.

My reason for sharing this story is to empower you to not just "think" but to honestly "believe" that most of your everyday, run-of-the-mill fears—of acceptance, rejection, judgment, failure, success, and so on—are totally and completely created in your own mind. And what you can create, you can also destroy!

Now, obviously, my singing incident came about because of someone else's request. I was going to say that it came about because someone "made me" do it, but you and I know that's bullshit. No one can make us do something like that. I wanted to continue forward with the really solid self-improvement stuff I was doing with the group, and I knew this opportunity came up for a reason. It just took someone else to set it up for me.

So, now you are me and I'm the facilitator. Let's take the first full baby step together toward that salad bar. In doing so:

1. You will learn how the universe is set up to practically hand you a fulfilled life.

2. You will learn how to be more self-aware.

3. Finally and most important, YOU WILL TAKE ACTION!

 **VIDEO TIME: VIDEO #3**

You've Got to Know It

(How to Build the Perfect S'more)

CHAPTER 2

The Rules of the Game

"It takes considerable knowledge just to
realize the extent of your own ignorance."

—THOMAS SOWELL

YOU CANNOT FIGURE OUT WHO YOU REALLY ARE or what
your life is about or how you're supposed to make your
imprint on this world, unless:

YOU KNOW THE RULES
AND HOW TO PLAY THE GAME

I've always had this radio-ish type of voice and the
innate ability to throw just total bullshit if the mood strikes.
So, a few years back, when I could actually fake *any* form
of dexterity on the basketball court, I somehow convinced
a buddy of mine that I was skilled in the knowledge of this
fine sport. I honestly don't know how because my dominant
left-handedness resulted in my only being able to go left,
and as a result, I mostly just passed the ball and crashed
the boards.

This assumption that I had any idea about how this sport
worked led my buddy to ask me to work the clock and the
buzzer at a basketball tournament his team was hosting. So,
like an idiot, I agreed, thinking I could be the voice of God

in that auditorium, finally having a captive audience that had to listen to me. Yeah, this was clearly a "take your ego to work" day.

The day finally arrived and, as I was taking my place at the scorer's table with a black box and a microphone, a high school girl of "gym rat" attire and attitude, dressed like a prison weed dealer and fashioning a tight blonde pony-tail, threw me a side glance and exclaimed in no uncertain terms, "Okay, let's go, it's time to make the introductions."

Have you ever had an experience where you found you have completely misread a situation, where the rug of your understanding has been pulled out from under your feet and you find yourself in that very "Wile E. Coyote just ran off the edge of the cliff and is suspended in midair before freefalling to the canyon floor" moment?

Not only had I never been in the position to make any basketball game introductions, I'd never paid attention to how it's done at any basketball game I'd ever attended. Basically, I had fake-charmed my way with a finger's tip full of natural speaking talent and a Chevy Suburban full of bullshit.

With the instantaneous flood of panic, my concern quickly shifted to damage control. *How am I going to pull this off, and more important, how am I going to keep from completely messing this event up for my buddy and the teams and the parents?*

Fighting off the inevitable tide of flop sweat, I quickly summoned my buddy over to me.

"So," I said with a weak mask of confidence, "how do you want me to do this? I mean, I could do this a number of ways, but, hey man, it's up to you."

Even thinking about that now makes me cringe. What

a line of bullshit. Although, asking someone for help in a way that comes across like you're asking for their expertise is an effective way to get solid feedback and reinforce their self-worth. And, truth be told, it did work. I got what I wanted—direction!

With my minimalistic approach to gabbing on the mic, along with a relatively uneventful game, no one in that gym was the wiser that there was a true idiot behind the mic.

This leads me to the point I want to make to you: In my basketball announcer experience, I was blinded by my Ego, thinking, *Whatever, it's just basketball, and I've "played it" and I'm familiar with it, so I can do this.*

More than likely, you are just like I was, sitting in that announcer's seat at that basketball game. You "think" you know what's going on because you've "played" it. Hell, you've played it your whole life. But just because you've played the game your whole life doesn't mean you know the rules or are even good at the game. There's a chance you're playing the game of life by someone else's rules, which clearly aren't written for you and your particular uniqueness. So what happens is, you really don't know how it's supposed to work and you find yourself bumblin' and stumblin' through life, listening to this person, then to that person, then a combination of what they both said, then completely throwing all that nonsense out and doing what you want but having no confidence because you constantly doubt yourself and your choices.

Then you find yourself going to church or synagogue or mosque, or signing up for a seminar and following "their" interpretation of what you should do with your life, but then that isn't you either. So then you read an Amazon Prime cart full of self-help books and get all fired up and then just mix and match all the different approaches without really knowing why you are making the changes, and on and on and on you go.

If you're reading this right now, you have some subconscious second-guessing happening about what the rules are, which, in all seriousness, is perfect because that means that you've reached the point where your inner voice (your True Self) is becoming strong enough to get you to start to question whether you really do know the game. Which also means you are not taking your Ego to work today! Great start.

More than likely, you probably don't know the rules. You probably don't really know the forces that are involved and how they all act and interact to your benefit.

I want to be mucho clear here. The Universe is designed to enable you to live your life to your greatest potential— full of life, of love, of abundance, full of success, full of amazing experiences, full of absolute kick-assery!

Here are the basic components of your life, along with a cute (I'm trying) explanation of each, and how they all can work together for you to make them your bitch. I like to call it the True Self Philosophy Model.

If you take a quick gander at the diagram on page 32:

◆ **Unity** is the Universal Energy, or God (depending on your lean). It surrounds and runs through *everything*.

◆ The **Big World** is everything that exists in the world around you, like other people, animals, trees, cargo shorts, Mario Lopez, etc.

◆ Your **Inner World** contains a number of components:

- Your **True Self** and your **Ego** are the main parts, and they're sort of like the angel on one shoulder and the devil on the other. They don't really play that well together, unless you come up against a legit threat.

- Your **Purpose** (the reason you are here) sits patiently waiting to be dusted off and wrapped up as your **Gift** to the world.

- Your **Vision** is the plan you will create to best share your Gift.

- Your **Foundation** is a set of solid ideas and character traits you need for your True Self to be able to clearly understand and support your Gift, and to then be able to craft a Vision plan to share with the world.

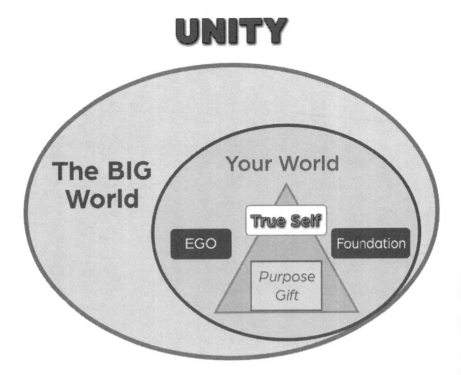

There you have it. That's the quickie bent-over-the-bath-room-sink-before-you-leave-for-the-party version. (Thanks, babe! Next time it's all about you . . . I swear.)

Because there's a lot of meat on each of these bones, I think it's important to expand a little bit more on each. Oh, and I suggest going back and looking at the diagram at the same time.

The Power of Unity

Unity is also known as the Universe, Collective Unconscious, God, Spiritual level, whatever blows your skirt up. Regardless of whether you consider yourself religious or spiritual or confused, the Unity energy fits without you freaking out that you are being led down a cultish path of internal fornication. I'm saving that juicy mindfuck stuff for the next book.

The Unity energy is *the* unseen force that connects us all. It's like interconnected roots of a thick forest of trees, underground and out of view, just like the Pando, a 106-acre colony of genetically identical aspen trees that is considered the largest organism on earth. The connection acts as an invisible bond between people that is based in an energy or relationship. Have you ever had that feeling that you just know something's going on with a friend of yours or you wake up one morning and have a certain person on your mind, and, out of the blue, they call you later that day? Well, those are two examples of the connective Unity energy.

Influences of the Big World

Everything that exists from your skin out—people, animals, plants, money, and In-N-Out Double Double (before consumption)—and your relationship to them all.

Your Inner World

This is the part we will be focusing on the most. It is basically you and your components, which are your thoughts and emotions, your beliefs, ideals, principles, your Ego, Foundation, Gift, Vision, Purpose, and True Self.

What Is Your True Self?

The True Self is part of your Inner World. Actually, to be laser accurate it is, well . . . YOU!

It is who you really are, behind all the walls and behavior patterns (Ego). It is the pure you that is experienced when you can just be in the moment without your feelings or thoughts being influenced by any past experiences or future concerns and/or anxieties and biases. It is the you who exists behind that judgmental voice in your head, the one criticizing you for just wanting to be yourself or trying to convince you that you aren't good enough or smart enough or cool enough to follow your dreams and Purpose.

The True Self is the you who was born whole and complete with pure potentiality, or with the ability to be the person you were supposed to be in this life. It is the light, or ball of energy, that burns brightly within you, also known as your life force.

Your Gift

Your Gift to the world is a manifestation or realization of your Purpose in the outside world. Or, to put it another way, it's the way you express your Purpose to other people around you and the world in general. It's not necessarily one thing or one action, but a way to represent your True Self by constantly acting or behaving from a solid sense of meaning that, with some solid work and practice, you will be aware of at all times.

This awareness of meaning will be your best guide to making decisions in your life that will keep you living with integrity and on your path.

Gifts can be tangible, something other people can see or touch, like a painting or a poem or a batch of homemade cookies, or intangible, like being an amazing role model or parent, teacher, helper, or friend. It is not a single act or action, but a continuous delivery of your Purpose to the world. It's what you give by keeping yourself focused on your Purpose in everything you do. Your Gift will be an "add" to the world, making it way better than if you were never put here to share it.

Since your Gift is uniquely yours, no one else can give it but you. That's why it's such a cool thing that you are doing this work right now because the world needs your Gift, ASAP!

Building a Foundation

Your Foundation is comprised of your core values, the guiding principles you decide your True Self uses as a structure to operate within. Any time I describe the Foundation to my clients, I use the analogy of a house. For your crib to be a safe, sweet place to crash and host your monthly naked Bunco Night, it must be on a solid foundation. The structure has got to be constructed well and with care and with the right materials in order for it to be a fully functional place to live.

Principles and core values like responsibility, account-ability, integrity, empathy, sympathy, genuine caring, optimism, and fairness are bricks in your Foundation. The stronger and more solid your bricks, the more unshakeable your Foundation.

A strong Foundation allows you to more accurately interpret things that are coming at you from the outside world, so that you can more clearly understand what's actually happening at that moment instead of being a slave to your past behavior patterns and overreact.

Let's say you get into an argument with someone about the best flavor of ice cream and she calls you an idiot because you like mint chip way better than butter pecan. Her reaction immediately triggers queasy gut anger because your dad used to insult you all the time by calling you an idiot. All of that past bad juju from your dickhead dad will now come bubbling up into your current discussion about ice cream flavors. (Most of the time it will be unconscious, which means you'll get super pissed but not really know why.) You may very well overreact by lashing out at your butter pecan–loving friend, leading to an escalated argument, leading to hurt feelings, leading to friend ghosting, then unfriending, and finally, buying the most expensive gallon of mint chip ice cream you can find and mowing it down while watching a movie you know she hates. All of this over an ice cream flavor.

With a solid Foundation beneath your feet, the aforementioned ice cream meltdown would have never happened because you would have been accountable for your overreaction and taken responsibility for your actions, which results in you operating in "integrity" with your friend. A solid Foundation will provide a high level of awareness, perspective, and consciousness in any moment of life, which will lead to a big reduction in pointless butt-hurting, as witnessed in the above ice cream drama.

Ego Is a Four-Letter Word

The EGO. It's the cause of so much life bullshit. Basically, it's the protective shell you have built around your True Self over the years that's made up of a group of reactions you automatically use in certain instances. The Ego has historically been defined as self-esteem, self-importance, self-respect, self-image, and self-confidence. However, I think those definitions are wrong and very misleading.

For the record, the Ego can generate positive feelings that may fool you into believing they are self-confidence or importance, but in actuality, those feelings are being generated to compensate for the actual Ego sense of "not good enough." These feelings are more in line with bravado or bragging or needing to be better (comparison), and in the long run, absolutely do not help you in the least. They continue your cycle of not being honest with yourself and are the real reasons why your Ego has to overcompensate. This comes from your automatic negative thought patterns that are created by the Ego to keep you from putting yourself out there.

Genuine, actual self-esteem and confidence come from the True Self. This is when you have that feeling that you "just know." Think back to a time when you were confronted with a problem and you handled it, right then and there, because you had this sense that you just knew what to do without having to think about it. Now think about a situation where you were confronted by something or someone and you felt challenged and a little uncomfortable because you were unsure.

If you "reacted" in that situation by saying something like, "No problem, I'll rock your world," or find yourself having to one-up someone to make yourself look better, then that's the Ego. Now, if you were in an uncomfortable or unfamiliar situation and you confronted it with more of a "I'll give it my best shot," then that would be an example of self-confidence coming from the True Self. My earlier basketball announcer story is a perfect example of this in action. My Ego was in control when I accepted the gig, and it wasn't until I faced up to the realities of my incompetence and asked for guidance that I was able to settle into my True Self and give it my best shot.

Along with the fake self-confidence, the Ego can also be that evil voice in your head that tells you you're not good enough or that you can't do something or that you're not attractive enough or smart enough, blah, blah, blah.

Let's say someone drops you a compliment, and, since you are not used to random compliments, you just dismiss it or deny it or deflect it or get pissed because you think they're just bullshitting or patronizing you. (I know—it happens to me all the time.) You think all of this instead of just taking the compliment for what it is—a fucking compliment.

What happened in this circumstance is that your automatic Ego response stepped in front of your True Self. It's like one dumpster fire after another, all the while your True Self is sitting behind the bastard Ego wall, screaming, "NOOOOOOO! Damn it, I do deserve the compliment, there is no ulterior motive, I am enough!"

The Ego consists of the basic survival instincts you were

born with, plus behavior patterns, prejudices, judgments, opinions, and automatic reactions you have adopted, mostly during the first few years of your life. And there is a pretty solid reason why we have our natural-born instincts and Ego: They are a part of us that we developed primarily for survival, or to protect the "self" from death.

A caveman, a tiger, and a priest walk into a Denny's . . .

Back in the caveman days, our survival instincts were an absolute necessity to guarantee the survival of the human species because, when it comes down to it, we are animals and are wired to behave cautiously so that we don't wander away from our luxurious caveperson bungalow to ask that friendly looking saber-toothed tiger for directions to the nearest Denny's. Some psychological and philosophical theories refer to this as the primal part of consciousness.

The "fight, flight, or freeze" impulse resides in this part of your consciousness in what is known as the lizard brain, the amygdala. This part of the brain has not kept up with the rest of our human evolution, leaving us with an interesting internal struggle between our larger, more developed "rational" part of our brain and our little, jumpy, overly protective and impulsive lizard brain. The lizard brain, the gatekeeper of our brain, has one job: to determine if what is happening in front of us is life threatening. And, if there is one whiff of a problem, it will boil our interpretation of the situation down into three possible actions:

1. Fight—Start swinging!

2. Flight—"Run, Forrest, Run!"

3. Freeze—You are now a marble statue.

That's all fine and good because it's a part of how we are designed, and it still really helps out when we are confronted (hopefully not often) by any life-or-death situations, like jumping out of the way of a runaway car.

I remember a good handful of times the gatekeeper saved me from either impending doom or at least a nasty head gash. But here's the rub: Once the gatekeeper decides what label to put on the impulse, it then sends it up to the big parts of our brain. (I would get into the specific names of the parts, but that really doesn't matter because neither of us is studying for an anatomy test . . . but for the record, I'm referring to the prefrontal cortex.) This is where the Ego and the rational thinking part of your brain tend to battle over who gets to interpret the impulsive signal that is coming from the amygdala. If the Ego wins the battle, it gets to work really fucking things up.

Since the Ego draws upon your past experiences and your current interpretations of how the world works, it is biased and very protective of anything that even smells a little off. I always refer to the Ego as a series of walls around your True Self that you have built throughout your life to protect yourself. Because the Ego is located in the bigger part of the brain, it thinks it knows way more than the amygdala and the True Self.

The Ego is that guy at the party who knows everything about everything, and, on top of that, is a one-upper. You know, anything you say, this douche-nozzle has already done it and done it better than you. The Ego is like a helicopter parent who keeps his kid in a little protective bubble, even when the kid is old enough to start exploring and experiencing things and getting in touch with who she is (True Self). That parent thinks he knows better than the kid, which may be true in some sense, but that's not the point. The point is, the kid is her own person and yearns to expand and learn and grow and experience, and the parent (Ego) is keeping her from her own life.

This is the in-your-mind crap we all have to deal with, every single day. You can see why sometimes we have such a hard time making decisions or keeping from freaking out over stuff that really isn't that big of a deal.

So the Ego takes it upon himself to be the decision maker as to how you process or interpret the impulse that has traveled up to your more developed part of the brain. And, since this dude thinks he knows everything, based on his past experiences and how he "thinks" something should be interpreted, based on the limited information he has, well, he ends up, most of the time, being the one who shapes your view of the thing that is going on in front of you in the moment. Basically, your Ego shapes your view of the world, unless you turn off your autopilot and begin to take control with your True Self. (If you stick with me, I'll walk you through how you can do that.)

Ego Example: Did You Just Call Me Fat?

Let's say you're chillin' with a group of friends, having a few laughs, chit-chatting, when the conversation casually turns to you. "Hey, have you been working out lately?" one friend asks. That question gets heard by your ears and seen by your eyes, which creates a signal to you that someone is talking to you and there is an incoming message. The first stop in the brain chain is the amygdala. In this situation, seeing as though your life isn't being threatened, it sends the signal up to the big part of the brain instead of rerouting it to your automatic reflexes to take immediate evasive action. Because in this case, you don't need to react, like having to jump out of the way of a speeding car or one of those racing bike idiots who thinks he's in the Tour de France.

Okay, so let's say, in this instance, life's been hella busy for you over the last week and you haven't been able to get to the gym or hot yoga, and you've already beaten yourself up for being a lazy fat-ass for not working out. The signal of the "compliment" reaches your big brain area, and the Ego is there to interpret the message for you. And, since you already don't feel that great, the Ego will interpret that signal to support your already "I'm a fat-ass" image and you will immediately interpret what your friend is saying as, "Damn, you're fat!"

Notice I said *immediately* because that's how your Ego likes to work—on impulse. It continually tries to step in front of your rational thought process in order to hijack it because that son of a bitch thinks he knows more than your conscious, rational brain when it comes to interpreting signals.

Bottom line is, the Ego means well, but it gets in the way like a hot-headed friend who is constantly overreacting, like Joe Pesci's "funny clown" implosion in *Goodfellas*.

The Importance of Vision

Vision is how you plan to deliver your Gift. It includes a *picture in your mind* of what the world would be like with your Gift and a general game plan to make that happen. The Vision acts as an end point, while the game plan is your equipment and the road map needed to get there.

A very important aspect to Vision is *flexibility*. It is rare for a Vision plan to go exactly as planned. More than likely, there will be many adjustments along the way. So, the point of the Vision plan is to keep the end result in mind while expecting the path to meander. Actually, the problems or roadblocks that present themselves along the way serve a specific purpose in the successful completion of your journey. The reason for the bumps and detours are rarely obvious at the time but will make sense in hindsight.

Please don't halt your journey to try to figure out exactly why this or that has happened; you obviously needed a path adjustment, so just go with it and trust the Universe. The biggest mistake we crazy humans make is stopping our momentum in those moments to try to figure out something that has no rational meaning. The Ego hates "not knowing." My favorite sayings in these moments are:

"It is what it is."

and

"Everything happens for a reason."

So get up, dust yourself off, take a deep breath, focus, and . . .

JUST KEEP SWIMMING . . . JUST KEEP SWIMMING!

 **VIDEO TIME: VIDEO #4**

CHAPTER 3

Your Perfect Life

"It's a funny thing about life; if you refuse to accept anything but the best, you very often get it."

—W. SOMERSET MAUGHAM

LET'S SAY THE NATURAL FLOW OF THE UNIVERSE and your True Self, Purpose, Gift, Vision, Foundation, and Plan came together, and you are completely dialed in. Here's what it would look and feel like:

1. Your True Self is already dialed into the Unity energy frequency, so your first move in this best-case scenario is to be able to shove your Ego aside and connect yourself on a conscious level.

2. Take heart in knowing that your elevated conscious awareness leads to being able to actually feel that Universal, True Self energy and to be able to actually see that you have a connection to a purpose. And from that connection you start to generate some pretty cool ideas of what your Gift could be.

   Your Gift can be anything from getting clear on a talent you have (like dancing or singing), to a skill that seems to come naturally to you (like respectfully arguing a point of view or solving complex math problems). Clarity through your awareness of Unity, True Self, and Purpose will lead to your knowing what your Gift (or Gifts) are.

3. As your awareness of the difference between the True Self energy and the Ego energy increases, you will become stronger and much better at ignoring the Ego impulses and bad behavior/reaction patterns, including all of those fun feelings that come up when you feel surrounded by idiots!

4. You will then begin to get even clearer on your Purpose and how to turn it into Gifts to share with the rest of us.

So, to recap: You discover your True Self, decide on your Purpose, wrap up that Gift, and map out the best way to share your Gift with the rest of the world. Simple, right?

Honestly, it should be, but we do a great job of making life so much harder on ourselves than it really is. It's crazy how much we get in our own way, subconsciously thinking we are protecting ourselves (Ego), all the while actually keeping ourselves from rockin' our life with our own uniqueness and taking action to make our Gifts jump out of our mind and into something that is real in the Big World.

So, this leads us to how we go about putting all of this into play and start kicking some serious life ass.

 **VIDEO TIME: VIDEO #5**

CHAPTER 4

Living the Dream

> "Do not take life too seriously.
> You will never get out of it alive."
>
> —ELBERT HUBBARD

I'VE BEEN SITTING HERE, OFF AND ON, for hours trying to come up with the perfect personal story to start off this chapter, one that will illustrate my own personal experience of everything lining up for me, like:

- Westley and Buttercup jumping on the horse and planting the perfect kiss, or

- Elon Musk changing the world of cars and space travel at the same time, or

- Finding a *Men in Black* memory flashy thing, turning it on myself, and obliterating any evidence of all Kardashians.

However, I really don't have a story for you, and there is a reason for that.

Most people will not be able to line up all of these things on a consistent basis to the point where they can legit call themselves self-actualized, when they are totally and completely connected to their True Self and they can immediately process all the shit that comes in so that it doesn't emotionally impact them. I mean, let's be serious, I'm not going to feed you a huge bag of Haribo Sugar-Free Gummy Bears (I could never be that cruel) and tell you that you won't slide into the pit of despair every now and again, no matter how "aware" and dialed in you are, because you will.

However, as you progress through understanding this stuff on a deeper level, the slide won't be as steep and you'll be able to understand and accept, at a much faster rate, the constructive reason that a crappy life situation showed up at a certain point.

That being said, I want to lay out the "perfect" situation. I like to think of it as the "in the flow" way of going through life, where you are completely connected to your True Self and are constantly in line with your Purpose and you don't stray from your Vision.

I'm not saying it isn't possible because it is.

All I'm trying to say is: **You must chill!**

It's a big, big endeavor to reach and then maintain that state of "being," and very few people have been able to come close to it. But that doesn't mean I shouldn't lay out what it looks like and set it up like a goal to shoot for because it is, and it's the main point of this whole book—King of the World, Jack!

Now, that being said, it's time to compare where you are right now to the "best-case" scenario (the way the True Self Philosophy model looks in its "perfect" form).

So, if everything was how it could be, and you were living the rock star version of your life, this is what your life would look and feel like:

1. You are completely dialed into your True Self.

Instead of letting your initial knee-jerk Ego response guide you, you are able to quickly realize that you are reacting from the Ego, and then you are able to make a quick shift back to your True Self, which does a way better job assessing a situation. This results in your having a more appropriate interpretation and then a more thought-out and purposeful action.

2. You have an insane awareness of Unity.

Modern physics (real science stuff) has shown that humans, as well as everything else—inanimate or animate—are composed of energy. Not to get full-on quantum physics on you, but it's the really fast vibrations of the atoms in your cells that create your mass. It's all about the energy, which can literally be raised and lowered.

It's like you're a helicopter. You can just sit there on the ground with no energy, takin' it easy, or you can fire up your engine, get those blades spinning, and start to climb to a higher elevation. And the more you throttle up, the higher the spinning frequency of the rotors and the higher you will go, successfully rising above the Idiot Horde. And think about how much more you can see from that elevation and what kind of improved perspective you'll have when you can see your life and all that surrounds you from a thousand feet up in the air. This is, no bullshit, the real deal.

3. You are aligned with your Purpose.

You'll be able to confidently own a sense of Purpose and know what needs to be done, or what needs to be changed in your life to stay on your path.

4. You have a solid understanding of your Gift.

In this best-case scenario, you'll have a clear knowing of your Gift, or what it is that you were put on this earth to share with all of us. Remember, though, the Gift may not be just one tangible thing; it could be a really good idea on what direction to take with your passion and talent.

People get too hung up on having to know exactly what it is they are supposed to do or create in life. Understanding your Gift is more about having a sense of what you have a natural knack for or where your flow usually takes you. This will light a fire under you to start a small project, which becomes a building block to other projects that reinforce your Purpose and Gift. It's a process you must buy into and trust.

5. You have a solid sense of Vision.

You will be able to connect the energy of Unity, your Purpose, and your Gift to a way of sharing it with the rest of us, and you will have the ability to sketch out a plan that allows you to share your Gift while balancing with your current life and the everyday stuff that comes along in the Big World (you know, the "crap").

6. You are proactive, not reactive.

This, I like to graphically refer to as "cutting the balls off your Ego." You will no longer impulsively "react" and "act" to things but will be able to quickly stop yourself, see things in the moment for what they are, and then be proactive, or able to take action based on your strong sense of self. It's about "responding," not "reacting." It's taking each moment for what it is versus letting people or situations push your buttons.

7. You have a Multiple World Perspective.

In the best-case scenario, you completely understand your view of the world is yours and yours only, and no one else lives in your head. The way you see things and feel things and hear things and the meaning that you give to anything that happens to you or around you exist only in your head in that exact way. Also (and this is a very important "also"), you fully understand everyone else lives in their own little worlds in their own little heads. It's not about completely agreeing with or fully understanding other people's worlds, but knowing that different perspectives exist frees you to accept the fact that they don't live in your specific world.

We function in relationships, groups, and societies with some parts of our worlds overlapping, like common opinions and habits, goals, or respect for common laws, such as don't kill anybody, children shouldn't smoke, and sexting your ex while on a date is *never* a good idea. Personally, there are a lot of "worlds" that I don't have a lot of overlap with and completely disagree with, but I understand that those people don't live in my head.

8. You are living in the Now.

Awareness or consciousness is one of the main points of this book. Being able to live in the moment, dubbed the "Now," doesn't mean forgetting past experiences or not looking forward to the future. Living in the Now enables us to take each instance for what it is, allowing us to accurately assess and fully understand the circumstances that form the setting of our actual, current reality, which is referred to as "context."

Living in the Now keeps the Ego on the sidelines, so you can see each moment for what it is right now and not have your viewpoint influenced by a past experience or a faulty thought pattern. The key is to use the lesson from the past experience to reconcile the unique circumstance of the present moment.

9. Your Ego is exposed for the stupid bastard it is.

You can easily see Ego patterns as they creep into your thinking or begin to play on your emotions. The ability to figure them out, then be able to see them as they rear their ugly heads, will keep the patterns from getting in the way of being your True Self.

10. You totally understand that it's all about relationships, not particles.

Dr. Richard Feynman, the theoretical physicist considered one of the fathers of quantum mechanics and one of the most brilliant guys ever (and apparently was a pretty kick-ass dancer as well . . . don't know why I know that), stated that the evolution of physics has exposed a deeper under-standing of how the world works:

"Relationships are more important than things."

It's about the relationship energy, the connective energy between things, and not the particles (the things) themselves. Understanding that *everything is connected* will heighten your empathy toward others and keep out negative feelings of isolation, loneliness, or victimization (as in, "Everybody's out to get me").

11. You embrace the power of gratitude.

The most powerful thing that connects Unity to True Self to Purpose to Gift to the recognized Vision is gratitude.

There's a great line by Konstantin Stanislavski, the creator of method acting, that states, "In every art we must have an unbroken line." To join all the inner and outer parts of your life, there has to be a connector. I have found that reminding yourself of the gratitude you have for being you, being where you are, and being put here to share your Gift provides a grounding feeling and plants you in the Now.

12. You are focused on fulfillment, not happiness.

I could (and probably will) write an entire book on why a focus on happiness really does more harm than good. It's not that being happy is a bad thing; it's just that happiness is not a goal. Happiness is an emotion; it's situational and relates to immediate feelings.

The problem is, happiness is being sold to us every day as the pot of gold to strive for, as in "being happy all the time." Such a misguided notion leads to a lot of disappointed people because that reality is impossible. People could very well come to the conclusion that they will never be able to achieve eternal happiness, which would lead to them falling into a deeper hole of hopelessness or to become more cynical or get more pissed at life. When you're out there searching for that elusive happiness and you don't have it, all you see around you are a bunch of happy fuckers who clearly don't deserve to be happy as much as you do!

So, here's the flat-out, no bullshit, truth of the matter: It's not about happiness, it's about *fulfillment*.

No, this is not just another way to define happiness. Fulfillment is about looking at the big picture and understanding that the expansion of your life and growth and new experiences and cultivating new levels of joy in your life include both good and not-so-good stuff, like happiness *and* sadness or disappointment or frustration.

Fulfillment doesn't mean you never have to deal with the bad. It's about being ready to deal with the bad, understanding and trusting there is a reason for it. Seriously, you need the shitty stuff in life because it has a purpose, and you have got to accept the setbacks, or terrible breaks, or the seemingly mandatory interactions with idiots as a necessary evil in your growth and expansion.

The focus should never be on trying to make your life as unproblematic as possible. The focus should be on understanding that any form of growth puts you in a different place with different things to learn and understand, and different types of challenges, and possibly more shit to deal with. It's about accepting the uncomfortable and, despite the crap, choosing to grow and expand and reach toward being a more fulfilled human being.

Knowing and accepting this truth, you can face all the crap head on, falling, cursing profusely, getting up, grabbing a snack, learning, growing, understanding, and ultimately expanding your life experience.

This is called fulfillment.

Enjoy happiness for what it is, something fleeting, but don't make it your ultimate life goal because you'll be constantly disappointed and stuck in your shit if you do.

 **VIDEO TIME: VIDEO #6**

CHAPTER 5

How Your Ego
Effs Everything Up

"Keep your friends close, and your enemies closer."

—MICHAEL CORLEONE, *THE GODFATHER PART II*

BECAUSE IT IS, LITERALLY, YOUR WORST ENEMY, I want to chat with you a little more about your Ego.

When you compare the "where you're at" with the model of how stuff should work when it all flows, you'll be able to see some areas where you're crushing it and some areas where you might be off. I've never worked with anyone who doesn't have some things that are pretty dialed in and other parts of their life that are not jiving at all. And the "not jiving" stuff obviously has to do with some lousy past choices or a current warped sense of reality. This warped sense of reality comes from our ole drinking buddy, the Ego.

Your Ego Is a Big Dick (and Not in a Good Way)

Right out of the gate, things go sideways because your Ego believes it is you—not just a part of you, but the whole you. So, any threat to its existence will automatically put your Ego in a heightened state of "look at me" and will immediately start yelling over the rational voice of your True Self.

Most of this comes from a combination of our brain patterns that were developed during the first few years of life, when our brains weren't developed enough to clearly see the things that are happening for what they really were: passing moments with very little meaning behind them.

Basically, as very small children we had a warped sense of reality and were making hard decisions on how the world operated, all formed with a mind that wasn't even close to being fully developed. So, what happens is the underdeveloped brain buddies up with the instinctual, survival brain (lizard brain), and what we get are patterns that exasperate mundane conflicts (arguments with coworkers, losing a job, spending the holidays with family) into struggles of life and death.

Like, say your dad bailed on you and your mom when you were just an infant (just an example, not an actual thing that ever happened to me that I've been dealing with my whole life). And as an infant, with that underdeveloped brain, you interpret that action as abandonment and, in a lot of cases, that creates a sense within you that you are not good enough for Pops to stick around or that you apparently don't deserve to be loved or are unlovable.

Do you see how fucked up this whole situation is?

In this hypothetical example, your child brain failed to see what the real deal was, which was the dad's (and I use the term "dad" loosely) issues and his inability to stick around and take care of his responsibilities. Instead, your child brain took the full brunt of the responsibility, and this warped sense of reality got imprinted in the mind as what actually happened. Because right then and there, the Ego stepped in and said, "Damn, I guess we aren't worth his love, so I better protect you from ever putting yourself in a position where you feel like you do deserve love because that person will just end up leaving anyway."

That's what the Ego does. Isn't it the best?

And, to make things worse, we as people are wired so we feel emotional death even worse than real death because instead of just dying, we have to continue to live and feel the hurt, day after day, relationship after relationship. And putting yourself in the position where another person abandons you is literally interpreted by your Ego as death. This is why it is very difficult and takes a lot of work to be able to consciously override an Ego program when it wants to be the first one to analyze everything that happens to you.

The most effective way to deal with these negative patterns is to first be aware that they pop up and then be able to *consciously* interrupt them. So, at this point of our journey, I invite you to think about the stuff that's not jiving in your life and some patterns you've developed based on inaccurate memories from an underdeveloped child's brain. I'm going to go through a few of the most common unproductive life patterns that people run across. You may be dealing with none, one, all, or all plus infinity.

Whatever the case, even if I don't mention yours, it doesn't mean that you can't correct it. That being said, check out the following beauties:

You create too much inconsistency in your life.

Are there things that are happening now that, according to the True Self Model of Life Domination, should be working, but for some reason are not?

Let's say you get up every morning and you do the whole "I'm grateful for my life and everything I have" chant. Then, still fighting off your body's unwillingness to fully cooperate in your mental joy, you work yourself to an upright position and drag yourself through your morning routine.

You go through your day with a heightened level of awareness, trying to keep yourself in the Now as much as possible as you try to relate to people, striving to communicate with them with the understanding that your perspective probably doesn't totally match up with theirs.

All of this should result in better, deeper levels of communication and connection with people, but you find yourself hitting the pillow every night with this empty sense that you remain unfulfilled. What the hell? You're doing everything that you're supposed to do. Why isn't it working?

Well, there is a reason or reasons why. In this instance, there's a good chance you are "thinking" about gratitude and "trying" to relate to people from their perspective, but your body language isn't matching your mental willingness to be more aware and communicative. This happens a lot because, like we've talked about before, *there's a difference between "knowing" and "owning."* Just because you have gained the knowledge of this expanded way of being doesn't mean your entire system (mind, body, Ego, emotions) are ready to fall in line and drink the Kool-Aid.

If you aren't getting more positive, more expansive results from making the alignment shifts we've been talking about, then that means your Ego is getting in the way, and it's a sneaky bastard. The Ego will let you think that, since you're aware of being aware and going through the motions of communicating with people on a more aware level, it is actually being played out in your behavior the way you think it's being played out in your head, when actually, your body language is not in line with your new alignment and that can be seen and felt in your energy by people, big time.

Most of the time, they can't put their finger on it, but people have this sense that you are not being completely genuine. I'm pretty sure you've felt that way about someone before. This is the result of your body language not matching what you are saying to people. It's like when someone rushes up to you, gives you a big hug, and, looking directly at you with a big smile on their face, says, "You are a loser, get the hell out of here!" Assuming this was an actual life scenario of mine, you could see why I'd be a little confused. The hug and smile were not exactly lined up with the words. (For the record, I've been called worse.)

The whole point is, you could be walking around, smiling and giving hugs, but your words and the smirk on your face add up to your not being fully aligned with the outside world. Most of the time, these inconsistencies come from fear, from something really scary that you don't want to validate or can't yet wrap your head around because it's a big thing that you have yet to confront. This is when there's a good chance you might want to talk to someone about why you can't make things work.

This is a HUGE thing. I'll say it again: If you are connecting with the concepts and want to expand, and, after working on it for some time, still can't figure out WTF is going wrong, then **GET SOME HELP FROM A LICENSED THERAPIST!**

As much as I would love to say I can help you solve any problem or you will be able to get through a big block just by reading book after book or going to seminars or buying smaller underwear to give you a heightened sense of control and increased band rash, it ain't gonna work. There are some problems that require professionals.

I mean, what if you have a significant problem with your car, one that even your vast knowledge of car repair couldn't fix. What do you do? You take the car to a mechanic, one who is a specialist in fixing the issue you need to fix. So, why would you have zero problem taking this piece of machinery in for necessary service when you are unwilling to do that with the most important thing in this world—YOU?

Taco Blocko Yourself

Another reason things may not be aligning for you is that you have done a great job at putting barriers up. Because, in all seriousness, we are our own worst enemies! Barriers are the excuses you are convinced exist and that keep you from doing the things you want to do. The key here is to become aware of them. Barriers can be stuff like:

- Using the excuse of not having enough money to do something

- Thinking you just don't have the time to do something

- Convincing yourself that you're in the wrong place or it's the wrong time to do something

- Believing you don't know enough or don't have enough experience

I'm talking about stuff that may seem like totally everyday, mindless stuff like scrolling through *HuffPost* and seeing an article that piques your interest. Its subject matter happens to be a passion of yours, but you end up skipping it with the notion of coming back to it when you "have more time," and, of course, you forget about it or keep making the excuse that you have "more important things to do." Then, one day you happen across your "saved" file where there are about twenty to thirty articles piled up, awaiting your attention. And the weird thing is, these articles are actually about something you have a passion for, or at least you are intrigued by the subject matter, or you wouldn't have saved them in the first place, but there they sit, having been shelved because you would rather thumb scroll through an endless time line of pointless or ridiculous "who wore it better" posts than focus your energy on digging into an article that may lead you farther down a path of self-discovery and fulfillment.

The thing is, these patterns are not just for big decision stuff. The pattern of "I'm not good enough or smart enough, or I don't have enough time or money" encompasses all of your decision-making. And the best way to "notice" a pattern is to pay close attention to your small, everyday decisions because—and this is sneaky—your Ego doesn't go into full protection mode if you happen to give a little extra attention to a small decision. And by small, I'm talking about stuff like taking the stairs to the second floor instead of the elevator or choosing the side salad instead of the duck-fat gravy fries.

The key is to be aware to a point where you have a "hmm, that's interesting" moment. That's the pattern recognition.

"The most exciting phrase to hear in science, the one that heralds new discoveries, is not 'Eureka!' (I found it!) but 'That's funny . . .'"

—ISAAC ASIMOV

In trying to make significant changes, especially when you're trying to make more than one significant change ("From now on, I'm going to get up at 5 a.m., head to the gym, drink liquefied endangered species protein, eat salads, and drink only tepid bathtub juice"), your Ego will immediately spring into action and do everything it can to make your life so miserable that you will literally be able to think of a thousand reasons why you "shouldn't" continue with the positive changes.

So the baby-steps way of starting to figure out what your Ego behavior patterns are is to recognize any type of trend in your everyday, seemingly uninteresting, daily decisions. It's almost like telling your mom you're going to the fridge to get some water when your intention is to nibble off the edge of the cake frosting on the last piece she told you not to eat. In a sense, you're sneaking past your Ego barriers and grabbing a small speck of knowledge, and, because you strategically nibbled on the edges, Mom was none the wiser. And, in the end, you will be able to successfully gather enough info to start to make sense of your patterns.

Who wants cake?!

You're Not Super Tuned into Your Inner True Self Voice

When you carry around a strong Ego, there's a chance you haven't yet reached the point where you are able to dial into your True Self voice or make it the consistent force for your thoughts and actions. It's like you've stacked about four shirts, three pairs of pants, and your favorite Dora the Explorer boxer briefs on top of your Bluetooth speaker so your sweet new Spotify station ("Songs I Will Never Admit to Loving" channel) sounds more like that kid in fourth grade who could burp the entire alphabet.

In this case, it's the Ego that is piling all the crap on the speaker because it thinks the volume is too high and will hurt your ears or the song sucks and it will bum you out. The Ego thinks it knows better than your True Self, which we know it doesn't. So it's time to take all those clothes off the speaker so you can hear Nickelback's Greatest Hit anthology in all of its glory.

How do you do this? A good way to remove the Ego and hear the True Self is to create an environment with no outside stressors, like a quiet moment alone with no distractions.

Although I'm going to talk about tools you can use to ground yourself later on in our journey, I do want to mention a sweet app that can help you create a calm, still environment. I highly suggest downloading the Headspace app. It's a free mindful meditation program that is insanely simple and takes only three to five minutes a day. I have found this to be a brilliant tool to introduce the unbelievable effectiveness of mindfulness mediation to anyone willing to chill for five minutes a day. I haven't yet come across anyone who doesn't have an extra five minutes. Seriously, check it out!

Okay, so back to my point: Once there's nothing in the Big World flying at you in the moment, you can focus on clearing your mind of any worries or concerns—past, present, or anxiety about the future—and then start to ask yourself some "who, why, what, and how" questions (I'll give you some examples later in the book).

The first few times I put myself in a place like this and asked myself what I want to do with my time on this earth, I had absolutely no idea. My Ego layer was blocking the process. Then, when I got close to discovering something, I would get really tired or antsy or actually get a big headache. That is the Ego's way of distracting you from getting too close to finding out it is a fraud and you should have been listening to your True Self the whole time. Although that physical crap distracted me temporarily, I didn't let it control me for long. I would sit back down again and go through all my "stream of consciousness" journaling and notebooks full of random, crazy ideas and even yellow sticky notes or restaurant napkins that were the only available instrument to catch a fleeting thought, trying to absorb it all as one big ball of information.

Basically, I was trying to understand the Big Picture, what it all meant and how it somehow was trying to tell me something, to show me "the way." It was like dumping out a 1,000-piece puzzle on the coffee table, flipping all the pieces over to the right side, then arranging the corner pieces so I could make some sense of how it was all going to come together.

When you create an environment with no outside stressors, focus your mind, and start to ask yourself some thought-provoking who, what, why, and how questions, it will most definitely form a connection with your True Self. The connection may not seem earth-shattering in the moment, and it may come and go depending on what's going on at any moment, but at least you know it's there, which is the important thing. The fact that you know actually sends a hopeful vibe through your system.

For the record, hopelessness is the worst, most destructive mind-set any of us can have. But the good news is, it doesn't have to exist if you don't want it to. This process of removing distractions and creating a wide-open space for some deep, meaningful introspection is the baby step into listening to and trusting your inner True Self voice.

With all of this self-analysis crap, I'm hoping you have a slightly better handle on where you are (why you're reading this book in the first place), what your barriers/patterns of self-sabotage are, and how you could be crushing it if you got your house in order. Now it's time to offer you a number of widgets you can use to elevate your game.

 **VIDEO TIME: VIDEO #7**

CHAPTER 6

Tool Time: Stuff You Can Use

"Life is like one big Mardi Gras. But instead of showing your boobs, show people your brain, and if they like what they see, you'll have more beads than you know what to do with."

—ELLEN DEGENERES

OKAY, SO YOU'VE COMPARED WHERE YOU ARE to the best-case scenario and you're able to see some strengths, weaknesses, inconsistencies, and even places where you are in alignment. You've also been introduced to the ways Ego patterns are created and how they really get in the way. Knowing all that, here are some great tools you can use to get more aligned with yourself. I have a bunch listed here, so take a look at all of them and decide on at least one that seems like a good fit for you and that you can start using immediately. Remember, the purpose of using one of these tools is to help you to get back to your True Self.

🛠 TOOL: Pattern Interrupts

A pattern interrupt is pretty much just what it sounds like. It is a mental or a physical thing that you can do to interrupt a negative thought or behavior pattern. This is a go-to move for parents of young kids, like when the kid goes into full meltdown mode, and in the midst of the inaudible *scrying* (screaming and crying), the parent yells, "Hey, Little Johnny, look! There's a doggy over there. Wow, isn't he cute?"

Most of the time, this interruption will cut like a knife through a pattern of meltdown and instantly get the child's mind on something else that does not induce full-lung screaming.

In terms of pattern interrupts, there can be two kinds: mental and physical. Once you have the ability to catch yourself in a moment where your Ego patterns are in full swing, the mental interruption is simple and you can start doing it immediately. My go-to example on this is with the numbnuts I have to share the road with.

Mind you, I clearly think of myself as a highly skilled driver who apparently has a level of competent driving expectations that are way too high for most people to attain. But seriously, I have done an insane amount of driving through the different jobs I've had, and the other people on the road and their lack of awareness and understanding of basic commonsense concepts when it comes to sharing the road drive me fucking nuts! This is a true "surrounded by idiots" scenario.

If you are lollygagging in the fast lane and someone comes up behind you who apparently needs to get somewhere in more of a hurry than you do, well,

MOVE THE FUCK OVEEEER!

So here before you is a quick look into one of my mental Ego triggers because I battle with being on other drivers' asses when they are going 60 in the fast lane. And, yeah,

I know I can choose to control my mental rage in these circumstances, and I do, eventually. At this point in my life, I've worked on it enough to only be pissed off for about ten seconds or so, with head shaking and furrowed brow as I make my way around this person. That's the best I can do right now, but I'm working on getting that down to about a second or two. I'm taking my baby steps.

Before understanding this concept of mental interruption, I would literally be pissed for days about how frustrating driving is when other people don't pay attention. And, in the end, the venting, the complaining, the ruminating didn't really make me feel any better; I just remained pissed until the next time I got in the car. That all being said, this is what I used to get all that shit under control: I chose a trigger word. Mine happens to be, "Whoa!" as in, "Whoa, dude! You're getting fired up over this person in the car ahead of you, and it isn't your own private lane, and you have no idea what's going through his mind or what's going on in his life, so back off and respect his reality."

I don't have to like the fact that this person isn't following the unwritten rule of "Move the Fuck Over," but I do have to accept that his reality and my reality can and should exist together and I really have no right to get pissed over someone else's choice. So I use "Whoa" to interrupt my inner Ego thought of, "I am being disrespected," in order to recognize that my Ego is boiling over and attempting to take control of my emotions and subsequent behavior.

The trigger word you choose grounds you in the moment and can vary by circumstance. Everything about you is aware and clear, dialed into the environment, situation, and people who are right in front of you, and with that comes a deeper understanding of the other person living in a different reality than yours.

As you know, whatever your buttons are, when they are pushed, it's go time! The energy is so raw and, most of the time, unexplainable, and there's a reason why. It comes from a place that was created when you were very young and the pattern was created by your undeveloped child's brain that sees things as black and white.

Your brain as a child didn't have the ability to really "see" things for what they were, and you classified some stuff that happened around you as bad or damaging or hurtful, or as a judgment that you are not worthy, or even to the point of something or someone being life-threatening. As we already talked about, these interpretations could have come from something as innocent as your getting separated from your mom in the grocery store where, after a short stint helping yourself to the "samples" in the bulk candy section, you found yourself wandering around a big, scary place, yelling for your mom. That scenario actually has the power to create an Ego pattern that you will have to deal with for the rest of your life.

I think our propensity for negative patterns is the biggest design flaw we have as humans. There has to be some way to structure childhood/parenting where that false imprinting doesn't happen. Can you imagine how many therapists would be out of a job if we could fix that?

Here's another example of a negative pattern that requires mental interruptions: Have you ever not liked someone on first impression because he reminds you of someone in your past? You may just have that "I don't know what it is about that dude, but I just don't like him" feeling. In that moment, you can catch yourself sliding into that mini-rage and interrupt the pattern by saying "Whoa" (or whatever your word is) to yourself, then look at the person as "not that turd from fifth grade who stole your lunch money." This little tweak can be done immediately and will allow you to be open to learning about the new person in front of you, instead of looking at him like you want revenge. This mental interruption creates a positive energy inside you, which will most definitely be felt by the other person.

When the Ego pattern is allowed to speak for you, other people will get that "jerk" vibe from you and, as a result, will not be as open or pleasant to you, which gets thrown back to you as shitty energy and then back to them and so on. I call it judgment ping-pong. It's a downward spiral into utter mutual contempt.

🔧 TOOL: Dr. Jekyll and Mr. Hide-Your-Ego

Another terrific mental tool for disarming a pattern is to give your Ego a separate identity. No, this is not so you can identify with your Dr. Jekyll and blame Mr. Hyde for all of your wrongdoings because that would be psychotic. The purpose of this tool is so you identify your Ego patterns, which, as you already know, are not your True Self.

An example of using both the mental interrupts and the separate Ego name goes something like this: I avoid Costco on a weekend like the plague, but I found myself in desperate need of a drum of olive oil, a two-gallon bottle of Kirkland tequila, and a chocolate cake the size of a truck tire. So I psyched myself up and headed over there, all the while knowing it was going to piss me off. So before I got out of the car, I attempted to ground myself with the understanding that everyone lives in their own reality, accept it, don't react, blah blah blah.

After about twenty steps into the building I started to lose my shit with the people who apparently check their ability to understand and abide by the concept of space and time at the door and proceed to abandon their Hummer-sized shopping carts in the middle of the aisle to peruse the free sample table to see which thimble-sized paper cup has the largest hand-broken, misshapen piece of Kirkland Natural Organic Grass-Fed Saltine Cracker. This adorable level of cluelessness immediately launched me into a WTF death stare along with an internal primal scream matching the intensity of that of a large North American woodland ape.

Perhaps you have had a shared Costco experience or have found yourself in a nightmarish circumstance, thinking the only outcome is either an under-your-breath "fucking idiots" grumble, a protruding vein and flushed face, or a good solid squeeze of the stress ball you strategically grabbed off your kitchen counter before you left the house. However, I am here to tell you that the "interruption and Ego name" technique works wonders in this type of situation. The first step is to give your Ego a name, by which you can directly address him or her. My Ego name is Donald, so when I am about to lose it, I say to myself, "Whoa [my trigger word], back in your box, Donny!"

This phrase and calling your Ego by name will help you separate your True Self from the sabotage your Ego is trying to establish. It reminds you that your reactions are not you, they are just Donald's uncontrollable aggression. This will redirect your energy and ground you in the Now, where you can accurately assess what the problem is in the moment and be much clearer about how to solve the issue without all the emotional baggage to fight through.

Fair warning, though, like anything, the hard part comes in knowing when and how to use it. But it's not that hard, and if you give it a shot and put the effort into trying to do it consistently, the technique will start to change the way you process stuff.

✖ TOOL: Physical Interruptions

Along with the two previously mentioned mental interrupt tools, there is a simple physical tool you can use that will interrupt your thought pattern. This approach is a little different from the other two because you are creating a physical sensation that you can "feel" that will snap you out of your current thought pattern.

Not to get all research-y on you, but this approach has its roots in a behavior modification technique known as respondent conditioning. And the cool part is it's really easy to set up and, if done correctly, will bug the shit out of you to the point that you will be able to shift your pattern without having to physically interrupt yourself anymore.

The most effective physical interrupt I know is the rubber band or the hair band (not the horrific music made by untalented fake hippies in the late eighties and early nineties). I say hair band because it seems like every girl with hair who walks the planet has a black hair band around her wrist.

Here's the deal: Find a rubber band and put around your wrist. When you feel your mind or your attitude slipping into a place where you don't want it to be, snap the band on the inside of your wrist. Also, if you catch yourself being a dick, snap the band. It's a very subtle process, and, more than likely, no one will know you're doing it. The more you do it, the more you will not like it, which will lead to you becoming more aware of your negative thoughts *before* they take you to an emotional crappy place, or *before* you act out and do something you may regret later.

I've used this technique, and it totally works. And, off the top of my head, I can't think of one client that I haven't encouraged to use it.

A couple of things about this: Make sure it's not one of those small bands that cuts off your circulation. The only time you should feel anything is when you snap it on the inside of your wrist. And, more than likely, you will only be able to do this for a week or two at a time. If just the sight of that band pisses you off, then it's working. That means it's programming you to be more aware, more in the moment.

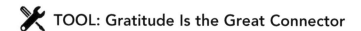 TOOL: Gratitude Is the Great Connector

"It is through gratitude for the present moment
that the spiritual dimension of life opens up."
—ECKHART TOLLE

I know we've already talked about this, but as a word and a concept, I feel gratitude does the job better than anything else. It's as easy as being grateful for the things you do have in your life, rather than focusing on the things you don't have because when you really give some time to thinking about what you have to be grateful for, I think you'll find you have a lot more in your life than you thought you did.

I find gratitude is the most effective concept to use to align myself with my True Self and, at the same time, to block out the Ego's influences and negative talk swirling in my head.

Robert A. Emmons, Ph.D., a psychology professor at UC Davis, is a big-time gratitude researcher. In one study, Emmons had a group of people write down one thing they were grateful for every day for three weeks. For a full six months following the study, the subjects in the experiment reported being an average of 25 percent happier. You know I'm not a fan of the "happy" label, but I think the results show a tangible improvement in what I like to call a "mind-set baseline," or the level at which your mind naturally operates.

I think Dr. Emmons nailed it with the following four reasons why gratitude is such a powerful tool:

1. Gratitude allows us to celebrate the present. Because positive emotions wear off quickly, gratitude makes us appreciate the value of something, and when we appreciate the value of something, we extract more benefits from it; we're less likely to take it for granted. Noticing the positives magnifies the pleasures you get from life.

2. Gratitude blocks toxic, negative emotions such as envy, resentment, and regret. To make this point, Dr. Emmons refers to a 2008 study by psychologist Alex Wood published in the *Journal of Research in Personality* showing that gratitude can reduce the frequency and duration of episodes of depression. This makes a lot of sense because we aren't wired to feel incompatible emotions like jealousy and gratitude at the same time. Also, other research conducted by Dr. Emmons along with Michael McCullough and Jo-Ann Tsang suggests that people who have high levels of gratitude have low levels of resentment and envy.

3. Grateful people are more stress resistant. There's a number of studies showing that people with a grateful attitude recover more quickly when faced with serious trauma, adversity, and suffering than those who don't consistently reflect on their own gratitude. Dr. Emmons believes that gratitude gives people a perspective from which they can interpret negative life events with a more realistic perspective, which helps them guard against post-traumatic stress and persistent anxiety.

Bottom Line: If you get nothing else from this book, I hope the concept of gratitude sticks with you. I truly believe this is *the* change you can make right now that will make the most difference in getting you dialed into your life and your True Self.

TOOL: Context and Why It Is So Important

In this whole process of understanding more about yourself and making changes to mastering your domain, it is of utmost importance that you continue to keep things in *context.* What I mean by context is to see things in front of you as they are and not what they seem to be.

Getting fired from a job or having someone not compliment you on a job well done or bombing an exam *does not* mean you are a failure or "not good enough." It just means that a particular life activity you did may not have turned out the way you wanted. Putting something in context means that you see getting fired from a job as an experience in your life, pure and simple. This is one particular experience, as is getting dumped or flunking out of med school or forgetting, again, to buy milk at the store.

Having the ability to put things into context will free you from defining your entire self by one life experience.

I'll say it again: Every successful person who has ever walked the earth has failed numerous times. They just happened to be able to contextualize their failures and use the lessons they learned to forge a more successful path. And the best part about all if this is, you have the same tool these successful people do. You have always had it; it's just a matter of dialing yourself into it, which, I'll be damned, you are doing right now!

In addition, having the ability to keep things in context allows you to start seeing patterns in your behavior and in the behavior of others, as well as how effective you are when communicating with a person or the world in general.

Use context as a way to see the hidden gems/lessons within every experience.

🛠 TOOL: Perspective

One of *Webster's* definitions of *perspective* is "the capacity to view things in their true relations or relative importance."

In the context of what we are doing, it's about having a grounded or acute understanding of what is going on in each moment and being able to keep the Ego programs from influencing that view. Viewing things as they really are in the moment is exactly what being grounded in the True

Self does. But there's a big chunk of understanding that's missing from the definition. It also has to do with having an understanding that *there is no one else on this earth that has the exact same perspective as you.*

This is a HUGE deal because once this concept sinks in, it really changes how you are able to deal with other people in a more understanding way, even with the moron who didn't say thanks when you held the door open for him at Starbucks the other morning. Seriously, who doesn't say thank you when someone does that? Whoa, there I just went!

Damn, you see how easy it is to go off the rails? But with my Ego pattern interruption of "Whoa" and my understanding of perspective, I'm able to more quickly ground myself and not let a little incident like that screw with my mind and tighten up both sets of cheeks. I'm back to calm and focused within seconds with the perspective of, "Maybe this guy just got some bad news or was bummed about his fight last night with his wife."

It ultimately comes down to the fact that each of us lives in our own world with our own very unique perspective and priorities. So, as a highly aware human, your first responsibility is to be able to clearly view your situation (understand your own perspective) and the second is to understand that everyone else has a different perspective than you do.

Typically, people tend to gravitate toward others with some similarities in perspective. I refer to it as an overlap in worlds. I'm talking about friends and other like-minded groups you may be part of, such as a religious group or political party or the small but handsome group of mall Santas.

But, on the flip side, I'm sure there's someone in your family or someone you know that you believe is certifiably nuts. In other words, there is absolutely zero overlap of your two worlds. Most of the time the separation of our worlds has to do with having a much different perspective on things versus being legitimately psychotic.

✖ TOOL: Acceptance Makes the Heart Grow Fonder

My favorite saying *ever* is, **IT IS WHAT IT IS.**

Some people really hate it, maybe because they want to wallow in a crappy moment or something, I don't really know. What I do know is the immediate acceptance of "what is" is extremely powerful, like an automatic reset button you can push without having to straighten a paperclip to reach.

Acceptance allows you to stop putting all that energy into fighting the reality of "what is" or being pissed or bummed that something happened. It jolts you into immediately being able to think proactively.

You see, accepting IS NOT about throwing your hands up and giving up. It's about moving or growing out of that static position, along with the knowledge of how you got there in the first place and what you can do to keep yourself moving forward. Acceptance is not being a "victim of circumstance," and it's not an excuse or a way to blame someone or something else for your current circumstance. Acceptance allows you to use all of your valuable energy to look for answers, to start the expansion and growth process again.

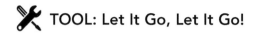 **TOOL: Let It Go, Let It Go!**

> "I don't care what they're going to say. Let the storm
> rage on. The cold never bothered me anyway."
>
> —ELSA, DISNEY'S *FROZEN*

This concept is known as surrender. It's a lot like acceptance, but it more specifically defines the amount of energy you are currently giving to something that you cannot change.

Let's say you're building a railroad and you map out a route and, whoops, there's a mountain where it wasn't supposed to be. At this point you can piss and moan and rip the mountain a new asshole as much as you want, but it ain't movin'. It is now time to surrender to the fact the map was wrong and you'll have to make an adjustment.

Being open to adjustments and having flexibility are two of the most important tools you are going to need moving forward. Remember, the Ego programs want to keep you stuck because it's safer for the Ego to make decisions based solely on what you know up to a certain point; it is not a fan of anything "new" or "thinking outside the box." The Ego will create a lot of internal tension so you focus on the stress and stay stuck (and safe) instead of taking a risk by making corrections and moving forward proactively.

Surrender to the realities of the moment if they don't match what you think should be. Remember, this doesn't mean give up; it means "let go" of the way you think it "should have been," so you can move forward on dealing with what actually is.

In *The Power of Now*, one of my all-time favorite books, Eckhart Tolle talks about dealing with a crappy situation this way:

"If you find your here and now intolerable . . .
you have three options: remove yourself from
the situation, change it, or accept it totally."

In all of those instances, it's about surrendering to "what is."

 TOOL: Mantras

I hesitate to use the word *mantra* because it may create a mental picture of some guru in a mostly white sheet mumbling to himself in the corner. (I would probably feel more comfortable if I could see his hands.) But I am using it because, it is what it is. Having a mantra means to have a word or short phrase that is powerful enough that, when said over and over, it will act as a powerful grounding/alignment tool. I have used a few, such as:

"It is what it is."

"They don't live in my world."

"Everything happens for a reason."

"Serenity now." (à la *Seinfeld's* Frank Costanza)

In selecting a mantra, it has to pack a punch, or in other words, it has to have *leverage*. It has to mean enough to you to cut through the Ego crap in any moment. Personally, as a dad (yes, this is a squishy moment), my daughter means everything to me. And as a coach/mentor/facilitator, I am passionate about understanding the world, so I can help others create an insane level of passion and purpose.

Since these two things really move me, my mantras have come from these passions.

If you take a look at the example mantras I've listed, none of them have my daughter's name in them, nor do they refer directly to my passion to help others. What they do have is a strong internal, emotional, passionate connection that I have given them. For example, when I use "Everything happens for a reason," I'm immediately connected to the feeling of always wanting to protect my daughter from the cruelties the world sometimes shines upon all of us. However, after going through the process of raising her, I understand that the sometimes crappy or painful situations that come up in life can serve as a valuable life lesson or a much-needed course correction. So now, by saying, "Everything happens for a reason," it immediately reminds me of her life success through some very difficult times and the positives that came from dealing with obstacles. For me, that is one of the most powerful grounding images I've ever created and I still use it to this day.

A number of years ago, I was fortunate enough to be selected to go to a weeklong facilitator's certification workshop. The primary goal was to work on one presentation the whole week so we could give the best speech of our lives. I went into the week with a good deal of confidence that I would crush the speech because I've done it so many times before. However, right off the bat, I was directly challenged by one of the expert coaches because I wasn't bringing enough passion to the table. And, as much as I wanted to fight his assessment, he was totally right. I didn't have enough leverage to move myself, let alone a room full of strangers.

The bottom line is, it took me the whole damn week to understand what leverage was and how it can completely override any Ego program when packaged into a very powerful and very personal mantra. No past Ego pattern or future anxiety can withstand the power/energy that your selected passions will bring to the fight. That's why mantras work.

So, for you, I suggest asking yourself the question, "Who or what means the most to me in my life?" The answer should come immediately to you because, typically, this is a truth that even your Ego won't deny. In all my time doing this stuff, I've never run across anyone who hasn't had something or someone out there that they don't care about, even to the point of caring about it/them more than they care about themselves.

For the record, if you can't think of anyone or anything, then you are lying to yourself. Take a deep breath, stop fucking around, and answer the question. By the way, the answer could very well be "yourself." Once you answer and find your grounding point, then it's just a matter of thinking about "why" they (or it) mean so much to you, and then your mantra will come from that. Can you see why uttering a short phrase that immediately reminds you of someone you deeply care about would have an emotionally grounding impact on you? That's why this tool is so effective.

🛠 TOOL: Just Breathe

Breath focus is a widely known and used tool to ground oneself in the moment. When you focus on your breath, you are focusing on "seeing" the air enter your lungs as you take a deep breath in, then visualizing the air leaving as you breathe out. For me, I use the visual of breathing in a light smoke or mist through my nose, then exhaling the smoke out of my mouth, letting it go. It simply involves putting all of your focus on your breath; that's it. As a matter of fact, the Headspace app I mentioned earlier uses breath focus as its primary tool to teach people how to integrate mindful meditation into their daily lives.

Just stop and listen/feel/see the air going into your lungs and out of your lungs. It is rather shocking how this very simple thing can block out everything except for "what is." Paying attention to breath immediately centers you in your body. It lines up the mind and body and puts you smack-dab into the Now. It's a great way to clear the grumblings of the Ego, reconnect with your perspective and priorities, and hear your True Self speak if you also choose to repeat your mantra during your breath work.

There is also another very effective breath technique known as "power breath" or 2-to-1 breathing. This technique consists of exhaling twice as long as you inhale, with all breathing done through the nose. Interestingly enough, this simple exercise is very effective at relieving hypertension, calming nerves, lowering blood pressure, and generating a strong state of relaxation.[1] The secret sauce behind this technique involves the sympathetic and parasympathetic nervous systems.

According to John Clarke, MD, in the article "Soothe Your Nervous System with 2-to-1 breathing" on the *Yoga International website:* "The technique of 2-to-1 breathing facilitates a deepening of relaxation by extending the period of parasympathetic activity within each breath. To put it more simply, 2-to-1 breathing decreases nerve

---

1. Based on the study "The influence of the 2:1 yogic breathing technique on essential hypertension" by Adhana R1, Gupta R, Dvivedii J, and Ahmad S.

activity in the sympathetic nervous system, which arouses the body for physical activity and exertion, and increases the influence of the more quieting parasympathetic nervous system, which regulates the relaxation response."[2]

So, by putting more emphasis on your exhale, you're basically fooling your body into thinking you're already calm and at rest, then it just thinks, "Oh, I guess it's time to chill."

Oh, just a quick heads up: Some people like to use quick breathing or multiple fast-paced deep breathing exercises to get in an elevated state of consciousness. Basically what they are doing is removing the carbon dioxide from their bloodstream faster than the body can produce it, which creates a chain reaction that leads to a dizzy feeling and/or disorientation. In a nutshell, it fucks with your mind, same as if you took some mind-altering drug. NO, I'm not saying exactly the same, but it does mess up your mind and can lead you to space out and speak in tongues or take you on a journey to find yourself playing naked Twister with your dead uncle Bob, that hot chick that works at Sunglass Hut, and a wise-cracking animated unicorn. Personally, I would stick with either the breath focus or the 2-to-1 breathing technique, if you want to integrate an effective relaxation technique into your toolkit.

 TOOL: Freeze

Freeze is about suspending reality in the moment. It means to stop everything from moving and see things for what

---

2. https://yogainternational.com/article/view/soothe-your-nervous-system-with-2-to-1-breathing, accessed September 26, 2017.

they are. It's almost like having the ability to stop time so that you can walk around and process everything that's happening in the moment.

So how does one do this without using the superpower of actually stopping time like one of those *Twilight Zone* episodes or Japanese porn videos (so I've been told)? Well, it may sound pretty lame, but it's just like you're playing freeze tag back on the playground in elementary school. It's about physically freezing in a moment, in the position you are in, and starting to look at all of the things happening around you (clock ticking, birds chirping, your dog eyeing you in silent judgment). Just the act of stopping and taking in your surroundings is a very effective way to ground you in the Now because it shifts your focus away from any issue or feeling that you're all up in, and puts the focus on the smallest things that are happening around you in the moment (hyperawareness). This is a great tool when you feel totally confused or overwhelmed, like trying to figure out what you owe on the group happy hour check when you had one beer and only a bite of the nachos. (I am *not* paying for any portion of Bob's five beers and the plate of poppers Megan ordered that NOBODY wanted!)

⚒ TOOL: Follow Your Nose

A proven scientific position is that our sense of smell is the strongest in regard to our connection to memories. That being said, tell me if you've ever been out somewhere and got a whiff of something that took you right back to your grandma's kitchen when you were just a snot-nosed hellion, or when you roll into someone else's room and it smells like total ass, just like your old roommate.

So, since smell is such a massively powerful, moving force, you can use this leverage by remembering a scent that put you at ease as a kid. (For your sake, I'm hoping your choice is not the room that smells like ass.) If you choose a scent with a strong enough positive memory associated with it, the smell will take your mind back to that positive association and, well, fool you into thinking you are back in that time, when you had a feeling of happiness or being loved or having fun. Basically, the smell grounds you in your True Self, bypassing all of the Ego crap.

TOOL: Create a Movie in Your Mind

This is a tool I learned in that seminar many years ago, and I still use it to this day. It's all about creating an image or a movie in your mind that reflects your desired outcome of a certain circumstance or how you want an event to go. It would be like taking a few minutes prior to giving a speech, closing your eyes, and visualizing yourself walking to the front of the group, scanning the room, cracking your first of many witty jokes, connecting with the audience, and seeing and hearing yourself successfully sending your message, with no hiccups.

A widely popular and effective sports psychology tool is for an athlete to visualize herself playing the game (or a particular move or shot) beforehand. Being able to see/anticipate things ahead of time allows an athlete to play more freely with less interference from overthinking.

Remember, the Ego hates when you step out of your comfort zone and take a risk. It thinks you are putting its existence in danger, and as a result, it will paint a picture in your mind of you not succeeding. Because if you succeed, that means you have just expanded your bubble, which will bring about more confidence, which will bring about more opportunities for you to try new things, which may put you in danger. How's that for circular thinking?

🔧 TOOL: The Magic Card

This technique involves writing down a powerful mantra-type saying like "I'm Batman" on a piece of paper or index card. The word or short phrase must have the power to immediately ground you or neutralize any overblown emotional state you have allowed yourself to get into. Then, you keep this card somewhere where you will be able to see it every day, like in your purse or wallet, in your sock drawer, on the bathroom mirror, and so on. The key is to put it somewhere you will see it every day.

At first, read it and give yourself a couple of seconds to own the phrase or process your saying. After the first week, don't read it, just glance at it. By just glancing at the card, you are allowing your True Self to take ownership of the word or saying without your Ego taking control and diminishing the power of the saying by creating doubts in your mind when you say it to yourself.

For shits and giggles, let's use the "I'm Batman" example. Let's say I write that down and look at it and "own" what I'm saying. And, as much as I would like to live in my delusion by actually believing I am Batman, that is not the point of this. That being said, I WILL NOT give up the cape! In writing that down, what I'm saying is, in a sense, I'm an empowered individual who wants to do good for myself and the world around me, and I'm not taking no shit from nobody! And, knowing that, when I write it down and read it the first couple of times after creating the card, I can actually feel what that statement says. I'm feeling all the badass stuff I just mentioned.

So, now that I've owned the statement, I just slip it into my sock drawer, word side up, and leave it there until the next morning, where I will see it when I go for my socks. Now, here's where it takes an interesting turn. There is a tendency for a statement like that to lose its power if you read it every day because you just get used to seeing it and when that happens, guess who joins the party? Your Ego.

After a few days, maybe a week or two, you will see the card and still get that tickle in your plums that empowers you and gets you into Batman mode.

But there comes a day when you read the card and in the back of your mind, ever so subtly, you hear, "Yeah, yeah, if I'm such a Batman, then why am I feeling crappy today or stuck in the same job or can't find a date?" The Ego will start to diminish the message by bringing up specific instances of not being Batman. It will try to convince you that you are not empowered or that reading the card isn't doing any good. However, there is a way to trick the Ego into thinking the card isn't there anymore, but you still get the kickass effect from your power statement. As weird as it sounds, you have to turn the card over so you can't read it. Here's what happens when you do that:

Your True Self already knows what is on the card; you don't have to read it thirty times to remember it. And, since it already knows what's on the card, just by seeing the apparently blank card gives you the Batman tingle, while the Ego just sees a blank card. Because, like anything, it's not the words on the card, it's the meaning you give them;

it's how you own your statement. And after a little while, all you will have to do is see the card, and using your power mantra, you'll reground yourself.

All that being said, I will let you in on a little secret: Some days the mantra will affect you more strongly that other days. This is a result of your normal up-and-down flow. Just because you get a Level 4 charge out of seeing the card instead of a Level 9 or 10 doesn't mean it's not having an impact. The impact is just consistent with your flow on that day or in that moment, so don't abandon ship if you have a couple of *mehs*.

⚒ TOOL: Carpool Karaoke

Music is an extremely powerful medium, as I'm sure you already know. I mean, who doesn't have a favorite song list, or ten, depending on mood and/or situation? To use this technique, you don't have to know how to sing or have any taste in music whatsoever. All you have to do is pick a portion of one of your favorite songs and write your own lines. Use a strong phrase or your own personal saying and drop it in the song. The song already has a powerful impact on you, you're already dialed in, so why not just frost that cupcake by personalizing it, giving it super-extra power for immediate connection? Let's say you're into Bob Marley and "Get Up Stand Up" fires you up because of the "for your rights" line. So, to personalize it, make a little change like, "Get up, stand up, I WILL stand up for (my) rights."

I know this may come across as a little (or a lot) corny or lame, but who the fuck cares?

At this point, you can even combine the movie-in-your-head tool with this one and "picture" yourself either singing the song or being involved in some dramatic reenactment where the song is narrating your fight to stand up for your rights. Wave that flag like you mean it, boss!

This lyric is happening in your own head, unless you care to entertain the surrounding unwashed masses with your own vocal rendition. But the whole point is to keep this part to yourself, and, that being the case, the lame part may make you cringe a little at the beginning, but, just like the mantra card in the sock drawer, you'll get to a point where you just have to hear the first beat of the song and you will instantly be dialed into your custom line, which will, I guarantee, bring a little smirk to your face. And, whadayaknow, you'll find yourself in a pretty cool state of mind.

 TOOL: Mindful Meditation

OHHHHMMMMM! That's my attempt at the sound of guttural chanting coming from some unsavory-looking, quasi-yogi bear sitting crossed-legged on a self-stitched hemp mat, in the corner of an incense-fogged room, wearing what appears to be a Goodwill purchased off-white bedsheet (dude, I can see the tag), chanting for an hour to reap the benefits of meditation. Let's just say, this is not what I mean by meditation.

Webster's Dictionary defines *meditation* as "a way to engage in contemplation or reflection for the purposes of reaching a heightened level of awareness; to focus thoughts."

Meditation is not a specific verb that means "crossed-legged for an hour"; it just means to put yourself in a mental state where you can focus and be more aware of the moment. This can be done almost anywhere and anytime, like the few minutes before you start the workday, while you're eating lunch, while you're sipping your coffee, and so on.

It just has to do with taking a couple of minutes to center yourself and focus on your relationship to your surrounding environment in the moment. This allows you to ground yourself and silence the Ego voice in your head that's stressing you out. It gives your True Self space to create energy and solutions.

There are some legit, researched, and verified health benefits to using some form of meditation on a daily basis. Also known as mindfulness practice, meditation can actually help decrease the powerful influence of our amygdala, which is that little lizard brain that houses the fight, flight, or freeze impulses, according to a study from the University of Pittsburgh and Carnegie Mellon University. Another study from the University of Wisconsin–Madison found that people who meditate regularly have essentially rewired the neural pathways in their brains, potentially leading to a more efficient brain when it comes to being able to pay attention, learn, and stay in a more heightened state of awareness. The good news is there are more and more studies that are coming out every day supporting meditative practice. And, nowadays, you can't go a couple of days without hearing or seeing something about mindfulness. I'm really glad to see the term taking hold and becoming part of the accepted fabric of our culture.

Not to beat a dead horse, but . . . use the Headspace mindfulness meditation app or go to Headspace.com.

🔧 TOOL: Use a Single Letter

This approach is like the magic card but involves just a small round sticker that you put one, maybe two letters on, with the letter(s) signifying a very powerful grounding word. For instance, if you constantly say, "It is what it is," put an "I" on the sticker. The sticker is a representation of the powerful grounding saying.

This is something that you put on your wallet or purse or computer, wherever it will be seen at least once a day. Just like the magic card, don't try to own the saying every time you see the sticker, just acknowledge the sticker and the True Self will do the rest.

Once you have tried out a few of the above grounding tools and found at least one that gives you the power to more consistently tap the energy of your True Self, it's time to start choosing what things, ideas, and concepts drive the direction of your Purpose, or in other words, to start asking yourself, How strong is my character?

The structure of your True Self consists of a number of concepts, freely chosen by you, that will keep you grounded and create much more consistency in your life. It's like building a house from a great set of plans with a really solid foundation and a super-reinforced wood frame. Do you see how the "tools" apply in this analogy? This type of structure is built to stand strong and not waver from outside influences. It's a safe haven because you built it strong—Strong Like Bull.

And, that takes us to our next chapter...

 **VIDEO TIME: VIDEO #8**

CHAPTER 7

Character: Building Your Foundation

> "Character is like a tree and reputation is like its shadow. The shadow is what we think of it; the tree is the real thing."
>
> —ABRAHAM LINCOLN

AS FAR AS GENERALLY ACCEPTED DEFINITIONS GO, *Webster's Dictionary* defines *character* as, "the mental and moral qualities distinctive to an individual." Like I said before, through this guided journey to figuring your shizz out, you first have to go through the relearning part, which is what we are doing right now, then it's on to the self-assessment of where you are now and where you feel you want to go (we touched on that a little and will get more into that in the next chapter). Then it's about putting all of that into motion and actually making it happen, which is the last section of this book.

Settling into who you are and what is really important to you in your life involves building up and strengthening your character—basically, deciding on what you stand for as an individual.

Think of yourself as an artist who just had a big lump of clay dropped right in front of you. Your choices on what that lump should look like and how you go about shaping and molding that lump is like you shaping and molding your character. It's you using your conscious brain to decide how to be with yourself and how to act toward all other people. That being said, the following are a couple of ways to check yourself to see if you are cool with your current depth of character.

Real Strengths and Weaknesses

Have you ever been in a situation, like a job interview or filling out a job application, where they ask you to list your strengths and weaknesses? Personally, I think those are horseshit questions because it's basically a setup by employers to see either how insecure you are or how big of a d-bag you can be. However, I think it's a brilliant move on your part to go through the exercise.

For the longest time, I never asked myself what I thought my strengths and weaknesses were because I never thought I had to. I mean, I am who I am, right? I think I'm a nice, giving person who does the best he can not to go postal on the army of idiots I run across every day. I mean, sure, I may have a slight weakness in not possessing an adequate supply of patience in certain circumstances, but overall, I think I do okay.

There's a chance that what I think of as my strengths and/or weaknesses could be straight from the Ego, which is not great. Those protective self-opinions could lead me astray toward thinking I might have a handle on things because it's a strength of mine, when actually I could be making the situation much worse, possibly pissing people off, creating mass confusion, or making a terrible decision.

So now, I give you the opportunity to explore your character strengths and weakness with a little bonus tool to figure out if any of them stem from that effin' Ego.

Bonus Tool: The Old Split-the-Paper Trick

Take out a piece of paper, draw a line down the middle, and begin to write down your strengths on one side and weaknesses on the other. Think of your strengths like the things you do or a quality you have that your best friend would say you have. It could be anything from being good at math to being a good listener, being dependable, or being loyal. Weaknesses can include things like a tendency to be late, a lack of patience, being gossipy, or eating crappy food.

There is no right or wrong way to list these. Actually, you'll learn a lot more about yourself if you just write down what pops into your head. It could be a word, a phrase, or a short story having to do with a situation that happened in your life. And when you have a few things written down, you can move to the most important part of this little experiment: Ego hunting time!

I Ask, Therefore, I Am

Once you have a list you can work with, stand up and stretch your legs, get a drink, pick up that thing on the floor you've been stepping over for a week—just disengage from the list. This is very important.

Now, this is the fun part: Once you sit back down, ground yourself with your new chosen grounding tool or tools—you know, the ones I just went through in the last chapter—and read each item on the list. After reading one thing you wrote, ask yourself, "Is this really something that reflects who I am, my True Self, or does this come from the Ego? Is it something that is a reaction to some outside influence, or better yet, is it something that bugs me for no apparent reason? For instance, is it something my parents always told me I should be or how I should think or what I should believe? Or is it a way of thinking or behaving or believing I have developed as a result of a lousy childhood event, like growing up in a household with a lot of conflict and learning to make it stop by becoming a people-pleaser?"

For any of this to work, you must be totally honest in your personal analysis. Hint: If there's some hesitation to writing anything down or if you feel uncomfortable or get that queasy feeling during this part, then you're on to something, so write it down.

Now, there will be some cases where one of your perceived strengths or weaknesses may be a foundational trait and *also* may come from a reaction or perception created from the Ego. So, you have three choices:

1. If it's something you consider an integral character trait of who you are, put a T for True Self next to it.

2. If it is an Ego program, put an E next to it.

3. And, if it falls under both, put a B next to it.

Don't think for a second that all of your weaknesses are from the Ego because they are not. As part of the natural law of things, we all have true strengths and true weaknesses.

An important guideline right here is DO NOT OVER-THINK THE ROOM. Your Ego already feels threatened because you are trying to pull its curtain back, so just go with your gut. Trust me, you'll know when there's a trait you "own." The Ego-driven traits will make you slightly uncomfortable, make you snicker, or even make you look away from the paper because you won't want to own them. The uncomfortable part comes from the fact that it really isn't you.

The strengths and weaknesses that you see as "both" mean that the traits are tied to something called a *nodal event*. This is an event that happened in your life that was super important, super profound, or had a huge impact on you. These are the times in your life that you really remember, like the first time you were up on stage or the first time you were rejected for a date or when you lost your virginity or when you felt the satisfaction of graduating. It's basically an event that really made its mark on you and remains with you in some form or fashion.

For any of the "both" traits, it would be a matter of understanding the strength of the trait without bringing along the reactional Ego part of it. Once you've gone through all of them, you will begin to see a pattern of the traits.

Desired Strengths and Understanding

After getting clear on your real strengths and weaknesses, there's a chance you don't currently possess a certain trait that you want or there is a trait you want more of, like confidence, bravery, empathy, etc. This is the time you can actually pick whatever it is you feel is needed to strengthen your Foundation and make it your own, and make it a part of your True Self. Make a list of the traits you *want* to own, the ones that will guide you through the ups and downs of your journey.

At this point, I do need to make mention of a few traits that have to be shared by all of us for the human race to continue to survive and expand. And, in saying that, I'm saying you have got to have these three traits locked down in yourself before you can create any real growth and expansion in your life.

Numbers 1 and 2 on the must-have list are *responsibility* and *accountability*. These are ownership traits, which means they center you within your True Self, removing the blame game from your behavior. Ownership and accountability are very empowering, and although both make life harder (it's always easier to blame someone or something else), it solidifies your Foundation and creates a positive character example to the people you connect with. If you had a magic wand, wouldn't you wish that everyone would be responsible and accountable for their own actions?

Number 3 is *empathy*. Empathy connects you to everyone else. It allows you to understand that everyone lives in their own world and sees life differently. Empathy allows you to accept someone for who she is without trying to figure out why she doesn't see things your way. Then you don't have to convince others that you are right all the time, and you can put that energy into developing your True Self.

Finding a General Purpose

The process of analyzing your strengths and weaknesses and implementing some other foundational character traits you feel you'll need going forward, including responsibility, accountability, and empathy, will create a sense of clarity that will, undoubtedly, show you the direction the arrow of your compass points. Connection to your character traits, your strengths and weaknesses, and the basis of them allows you to consistently tune out the crap that your Ego voice is trying to feed you, which will, in turn, give you the space to hear a general purpose.

The general purpose will look something like, "help kids," "be the best parent I can be," "be a role model for my community," "change the world," "discover a cure," "be a positive influence in a big corporation," etc. It's important to "own" a general purpose before starting to get specific. Usually, your specific Purpose(s) will fall in line with your natural Gift(s), like "apply my love for teaching to help everyone I instruct to become empowered to discover the things that give meaning to their lives."

The ability to connect with the True Self allows you to create a solid, consistent Foundation. And when you dial into your character traits and start to live every day with a solid game plan on what you are all about, then, interestingly enough, you'll start to see some paths of purpose exposing themselves. Once you begin to create situations in your life that charge your batteries, you can start to explore your new curiosities by planning and taking baby steps, and by completing a small, fun project, just like what we're going to do together by the end of this book.

 **VIDEO TIME: VIDEO #9**

STEP 2

You've Got to Own It

(Drain the Bathwater, Keep the Baby)

CHAPTER 8

Freeze, Fothermucker!

> "If you could kick the person in the pants
> responsible for most of your trouble,
> you wouldn't sit for a month."
> —THEODORE ROOSEVELT

NOW THAT I'VE HIT YOU WITH SOME KNOWLEDGE about how the world works inside you and all around you in Step 1, it's time to move on to Step 2, which is to literally play the freeze game with your life right now, stopping all parts of your life in order to see what is going on around you. It's like using the Freeze tool I mentioned a couple of chapters ago, but on your entire life system, instead of just as a means to get hyperaware in the moment.

More than likely, there will be some things you know already are not good, some things you had a "feeling" aren't that great, some things that kick ass, some things that you maybe have a *meh* feeling about that are actually good for you, and some things you just don't realize you are doing to yourself. It's time to take your newfound smarts and look at your life from a more aware perspective.

Welcome to the REAL WORLD!

How the Hell Do You Get to Phoenix?

There's a well-told story about some dude being blindfolded and dropped in the middle of the desert with instructions to find Phoenix, Arizona. And the only way that can happen is if he first figures out where he is so he can chart a course.

This, my friend, is the part of the show where you have to, literally, freeze-frame your life.

Now, it's one thing to just say, "Freeze!" and have everything hang in suspension in a particular moment so you can make your way through different facets of your life (see the Freeze tool in Chapter 6). But that is only the first step of the freeze. The most important step is being able to see the things around you, and by see, I don't mean just saying, "Huh, would you look at that, my life is a fucking dumpster fire!" What I mean is coming to terms with the fact that you've made some shitty choices up to this point that have taken you away from who you really are and what you really should be doing with your life (remember accountability and responsibility?).

The point of the freeze step is for you to be able to take a good, hard, honest look at the parts of your life that you have created (it's all you, man; no victim mentality, please). Hey, don't forget the positive part of this as well, which is just as important as being able to see the parts that don't work. For instance, just the fact you're sitting here and sharing this moment with me right now is a sweet move on your part because you've reached a point in your life where you know something just doesn't feel right, or there's something more to your life than what you've experienced so far and you want answers—FAST!

This is YUGE! Do you know how many people actually

get to this point? How many people actually have the ability to see or feel that they are living a current life that doesn't fit?

So, I want you to just take a deep breath, hold it, slowly let it out . . . c'mon, let it out! I will not be held responsible if you pass out. That's a shitty excuse to stop reading.

Okay, do me a serious solid right now and, as you are reading this, look up off this page, straight ahead, then do a sexy slow-mo turn of your head to the left, to the right, and behind you. Just take in the room right now, and then come back here.

Now, tell me what you saw.

It may not seem that big a deal, but you just took a really big step. You just suspended your life and were able to look at it as a freeze-frame moment and were able to see a number of things that I'm thinking you may not have seen before. And, if you feel like you really didn't see anything, keep practicing.

Now, at this point with my clients, I have them answer a few questions to get the mind flowing. The questions are basic and are structured to bring out some thoughts you have that you may not know about. What I'm trying to do is expose to you certain patterns in your life.

The questions also are a little tricky in that how you answer a question says a lot. Which questions are easier or harder to answer and even how much pressure you put on your pen or how legible you write are indicators of crappy Ego programs trying to keep you down.

At this point I would highly suggest grabbing a pen and some paper or at least plunking yourself down in front of the computer and opening up a blank page to write on. I want you to take a look at these three questions and give them a little thought. Just committing a moment to think about them is actually doing what you set out to do, or what I want you to do, which is to freeze and take a look at your life.

1. What feeling or thought or event led you to reading this book right now?

2. If you had a magic wand, what one thing would you change in your life right now?

3. What would be a time or experience where you felt the greatest fulfillment?

You May Just Know What You Don't Know

I used to be the king of "I don't know." It's such a great response, basically keeping me untethered from any possible commitment of thought or opinion. However, in the process of being a huge ball of wish-wash, I ended up stuck in the land of indecisiveness and noncommitment.

"I don't know" is acceptable in certain situations because, let's be honest, you may not be consciously aware of everything and there may be a time and place where someone asks you something you really have never thought about or something that's way out of your wheelhouse, like, "How does one split an atom?" or "Why is the cereal called Grape Nuts when it has neither grape nor nuts?" I found that a lot of times, I would actually get a gut feeling about the answer to the question before ending up with "I don't know."

I know that if I can have a gut reaction to a question, it's poking something that I either don't want to wake up or that is already sore from too much use.

That brings us to the three basic questions I asked earlier. Did you respond with "I don't know," or did one or all of the questions fire you up a little, almost like giving you a chance to affirm to yourself that, "YEAH, I really want to do this"?

Understanding the exact reasons why you answered the way you did or how you answered is not really the important part. The important part is accepting your answers or your non-answers as a sign of what you may be clear on and what you might be fighting. I would suggest keeping those questions and answers around throughout the rest of our journey here because, as things progress, your answers might become clearer.

 VIDEO TIME: VIDEO #10

CHAPTER 9

Self-Inventory Time

> "People may hate you for being different and
> not living by society's standards, but deep down
> they wish they had the courage to do the same."
>
> —KEVIN HART

WITH THE NEWLY DISCOVERED INFO from your "freeze your life" exercise fresh in your head, don't get up and take a piss or make a sandwich right now. You have got to take this moment to dig a little deeper into the lousy mental programs you have that are literally holding you back from living the life you want.

Take a quick gander at these tricks that will give you the ability to gain a little insight into your stuff. If you want, grab a pen and paper and go to town. And, if not, that's cool because you will invariably do a little yellow pad work in your head just by looking at these exercises.

All right, here we go . . .

Chew Before Swallowing

So, tell me, Felicia, do you allow your True Self to be defined by the outside world? For example:

◆ Do you let the perception of other people's attitudes toward you control how you feel about yourself?

- Do you judge or compare yourself to others in any way? (Physically, financially, etc.)

- Do you define yourself by your position in your company? (When asked, "Tell me about yourself," you respond, "I am a . . .")

- Do you define yourself by where you live, what you do, your education, your religious affiliation—anything that exists outside of your Inner World?

Unless you are lying through your ass, your answer will be yes to one or more of these questions. The point is to recognize that, over the years, you have given *unbelievable* power to other people, things, and situations to define who you are.

The most useful part of this awareness exercise is the ability to recognize these forces right now and, in going forward, to try to catch yourself when you give up your own identity to something or someone that has nothing to do with your True Self. For example, just like we talked about in Chapter 2, in "Ego Is a Four-Letter Word," that Ego inner voice is making you feel like a failure because you got fired or weren't recognized for something you did or were told you're acting foolishly or stupidly, which means you're actually letting someone else or an event dictate how you feel about yourself.

Does the Carpet Match the Drapes?

In looking at and/or thinking about your answers to the questions I posed in the last chapter, I ask you, are your actions consistent with your dreams? In a typical FML week, is there anything that reinforces who you are or who you want to be? For instance, if you know your current job sucks, are you doing anything during the week to find a new job or learning a new skill to find a different kind of job?

Looking at consistency gives you a really good idea of how far away you are, right now, from empowering your True Self to take the reins from the Ego and align you to the life you want and deserve—that is, actually doing something about your life to create real change. I mean, you are the captain of your own ship, so, why aren't you steering in the direction you want to go?

The Answer Lies in the "How," Not the "What"

Take a really good look at "how" you answered the questions.

- Did some answers come easy, some hard, and some not at all?

- Did you press harder on the paper or use capital letters at certain points?

- Did you write more legibly in some places than others?

- Did you allow yourself to think about one question more than the others?

- Did you have a sense of dread or have any feeling of resistance in even beginning to answer any of the questions, like starting to yawn, getting distracted by something in the room, or getting antsy and having to get up?

If you said yes to any of these, you are actively running up against an Ego pattern that is very uncomfortable with the question(s). These observations are important in figuring yourself out. Typically:

1. The harder you found it to write or to come up with a solid answer, the more powerful the blocking pattern.

2. If you are pressing harder or using capital letters, it's a sign of conviction to what you wrote or a way that your True Self is trying to power past your patterns. (If you are on a laptop, then using caps or unique spacing or quotes or bold or italics would signal a heightened conviction.)

3. Less legibility tends to show a level of fear to commit to what you are writing or could be a lack of connection or interest in what you're writing. (On a laptop, this would look like your sentence trailing off to gibberish or into something that, if you took a couple of days and picked it up and read it again, you'd immediately call "bullshit" on yourself.)

A lot of times, people will not fully invest in answering the question if they don't know the reason for the question in the first place.

Time for a Recap

Let's once again recap what we've been through so far before moving on to the next, most important step in the journey.

NOTE: I wrote the following with the purple anthropomorphic tyrannosaurus rex Barney's voice in my head . . . your inner voice may vary.

Remember, the first big step was learning about the forces of life around you and the difference between your

Inner World and the Big World, and about gratitude and Vision and Purpose and that son of a bitch, Ego. In the process of learning about these forces, the clear takeaways (hopefully) were:

- Your biggest fears are created by YOU and can be conquered by YOU (see Chapter 1).

- There are rules to life that must be known and followed in order for you to have the expanded, experiential, freaking beautiful experience you want.

- Your Ego means well but gets in the way and fills your head with all sorts of nonsense to keep you from taking risks and expanding.

- You can absolutely align all of your life forces to create a deep sense of knowing who the hell you are and what you choose to do with your life.

- Relationships are more important than things, and gratitude connects your True Self to your Purpose and keeps you focused in the Now.

- You have a lot of tools at your disposal to get yourself aligned with your True Self.

- Developing your character is essential in creating a solid Foundation for you to work and expand from.

- You have to be honest with yourself and figure out where you are at right now before you can start to make any changes.

- You have a few tricks you can use to expose those lousy mental programs that have been keeping you from the life you want (see Chapter 6).

So that takes us to the last step of the $3^1/_2$ step process, which is all about taking action. Like I mentioned at the beginning of our journey, none of this shit means anything unless you want to do something with it. That's why I structured the book in a way that would get your mind thinking about something that could be a fun little first baby step that would speak to your inner passion or Purpose.

And again, I say with great enthusiasm . . .

Don't freak out or shut down because you don't think you've figured anything out.

You actually have, but you're probably putting too much pressure on yourself to know who you are or what your Purpose is. Newsflash: Something this big takes time to develop. But it can't be developed unless you invest in your discovery process, which includes reading this and thinking about the stuff I threw at you, and going through a little action step thingy at the end to actually prove to yourself that you can start and finish something with a sense of conviction and a deep knowing that it's a solid baby step to your making choices that line up with creating the life you want to live.

Word vomit over. Time to make it happen!

 **VIDEO TIME: VIDEO #11**

STEP 3

Time to Live It

CHAPTER 10

It's Time to Drop the Mentos into the Coke Bottle

"Don't become something just because someone else wants you to, or because it's easy; you won't be happy. You have to do what you really, really, really, really want to do, even if it scares the shit out of you."

—KRISTEN WIIG

AT THIS POINT, YOUR "MORE AWARE" INNER SELF is now waiting backstage, ready to share its new makeover with the studio audience that is anxiously waiting on the other side of the curtain.

This is the point in the program where it's time to funnel this stuff into an idea for a small action you can take, then "do" the baby step where you actually create something to show yourself that the last few days of plugging through this book was actually worth it. Your project will be an action or a creation that is a cool little expression of, basically, you being you.

Another newsflash: There's a good chance you're already rationalizing in your mind that you don't have to go through this step, that just by reading, you've learned something and that's all you wanted from the book, or that you don't have to prove to anyone that you have a better handle on things now than you did before going through the book. Technically, I like to refer to these Ego-generated thoughts as:

BULLSHIT

Have you ever actually read the instructions on spot remover or carpet cleaner? They say you should try the cleaner on a small area first to see if it works, or more accurately, to see if it might actually make the stain worse. That's what this is all about, using the tools and techniques and knowledge gained and trying them in some small corner of the carpet. Because if you don't take what you've learned and "apply" it while it's fresh, then what the hell is the point of the time you've invested in this book, or in any other book for that matter?

Don't work yourself up about this. In actuality, because you've done the groundwork up to this point, putting together an action plan and making something happen will actually be a very fulfilling experience. But, even though that's the case, your Ego will push against it because it knows that if you do even some small thing from a very aware and True Self perspective, it will lose some of its power to control you, so it will fight for its existence. That's why I have set this whole thing up so that your first action will be just a small baby step—so small, in fact, that you probably won't even consider it to be a meaningful action at all.

So, do yourself a huge favor and stick with this through the Action-Creation Phase. I promise it won't hurt (unless you want it to, you sick bastard).

At this point I'm going to guide you through getting your mind right to help you decide on a project idea and how to make it happen. If you don't have a clear idea for a project at this point, no worries. With all the stuff I threw at you so far, you might feel like you're in the weeds. That is why I'm going to go over the stuff I'm going to go over with you right now, stuff like remembering who you are doing this for and knowing your audience and ways to more effectively relate to people and take better care of yourself. And I'll also introduce some tools you can use to keep grounded through the process, like how to make an effective vision board and how much journaling can help you.

I would like for you to start to think about something that interests you. It doesn't have to be some mind-blowing passion, just something that brings that trademark smirk to your face or gets your head slightly nodding as you think about it. Keep that interest in mind as you go through these guiding concepts, and, more than likely, you will be able to generate some ideas about what type of baby-step exercise you can base your interests on.

I have found it helpful to my clients to jot down some thoughts as they consider the following suggestions.

Remember Who This Is For

Of course you are doing all of this for you, first and foremost. I don't consider that egotistical at all because of one very important distinction: The end result of your living a fulfilled life is that everyone else gets the benefit as well.

You are constructing your Vision plan to take action to create something to be shared with the Big World. Your action is an offering whereby you are making the world a better place. It doesn't matter if this offering of yours positively impacts one person or a billion people; it's still an offering, and you are still sharing that positive energetic flow so that others can benefit. For the purposes of this baby-step exercise, it's important to focus on sharing with maybe one person or a small group of people. At this point, ask yourself if there is someone or some group of people you would like to positively impact in some way.

Like I said, we need to make this action step small so it doesn't freak the Ego out very much, but will still be impactful enough to create some solid internal momentum in you so you feel more empowered for bigger future projects. So, in crafting your Vision for this step, it's very important to know your audience.

Know Your Audience

This is a process of trying to figure out how your Gift can best fit, or best be delivered, based on the characteristics that lie in the Big World that surround you (or in this case, who your specific audience is). Think about it: If your Gift happened to be, let's say, brilliance in math, but you found the world around you pretty much full of first graders, you would have to craft your Vision—communicate your Gift— in a way they could understand and use to further their own life expansion. I mean, you can try to present all your fancy formulas and algorithms to these darling six-year-old monsters, but that will prove to be a huge waste of time and, I'm thinking, will end in some form of juice-spilling rebellion, likely followed by intermittent sobbing . . . and that's no way to act in front of children.

Yeah, it would be really simple to deliver your Gift if everyone lived in the same world you do, but, unfortunately, no one does. And, spoiler alert: The more aware you become of yourself and how the world operates around you, the bigger the gap between you and most people there will be (wow, had a small Yoda moment there). So, make sure you take into consideration the personality and perspective of the person or group so you can create a project that they can connect with. Effectively understanding the difference between you and your audience is what I like to call *bridging*.

This bridging thing is all about being true to yourself, to who you are, while at the same time effectively interacting with the Big World, or more specifically, with other people. Picture it like you are keeping one foot in your Inner World and one foot in the Big World. If you don't bridge the gap between these two worlds, then you'll find yourself super pissed or depressed or at a point where you just give up trying to figure things out because, if you have both feet in your world, you will lack the ability to relate to people around you. You will not have the empathetic connection to others that you will need for a balanced, fulfilled life. This is the type of person who may be considered a weird genius, a person with a solid Gift to give or share but a lack of connection or the ability to communicate with other people that makes sharing the Gift impossible. You'll come on too strong and people will think you're a nutjob.

On the other hand (or in this analogy, foot), both feet in the Big World is just as bad. This manifests as someone who is a wishy-washy sellout with no original thought and a yearning just to fit in or to be accepted, or to just be one of those people who no one pays attention to; no rocking the boat with this type of person. This plain white "T" type of person has a complete lack of a sense of his True Self. He is someone who is reactionary and walks through life on eggshells, so worried about what other people may say and think that he is unable to even figure out his Gift, let alone share it. Even if this type of person has some notion of what his Gift is, he is way too scared to share it.

So, obviously, the best pick is the bridging option. If you can "have a solid sense of your True Self"—one foot in your Inner World—and plant your other foot in the Big World, understanding that everyone else lives in their own world and not be reactionary to their energy, then you will be able to roll along and not be negatively impacted by the feeling that you are surrounded by idiots.

Be the Smartest One in the Room by Learning How to Listen

An important aspect of bridging is being able to understand the people around you to the best of your ability. One of the best ways to do that is to really listen to them. Active listening is not a natural thing for any of us, but it is seriously important in connecting with others. It's the process of listening with every molecule of your being, keeping your mind clear of judgments or questions while listening to someone. Personally, when I find myself consulting someone or in any instance where I have committed to actively listening to someone, I use the breath focus technique discussed in Chapter 6. When I am able to just be with a person and truly listen, it's amazing how full the conversation becomes.

When successfully pulled off, the people you're talking to (or in this case, listening to) start to actually glow with confidence because they feel you are present with them, which gives them a deeper sense of worth, or a sense that what they are saying matters. Give it a shot. It will take a little time and effort to sink in, but it's totally worth it in the long run.

Eat and Grow Rich

Unless you are currently undergoing the *foie gras* diet and are being force-fed through a tube until your liver engorges or are experimenting with the whole human centipede thing, then you have complete control over what you eat and drink. And, since what you eat is at least 85 percent responsible for you looking good and feeling good, it's pretty much a no-brainer that you have the ability to get your physical stuff in balance.

For the record, if I don't work out on a consistent basis or I go on a Pop-Tart and Yoo-hoo bender, I start to feel like total shit. I get pissed at myself for making crappy choices, and, since my body chemistry is all fucked up, I slip into a really bad place, where everything (inner and outer world) starts to look and feel like it sucks. Then the Ego chimes in about how bad things "appear" to be, and then I think, *Well, if all this shit that I'm doing doesn't matter anyway, then, FUCK IT! I might as well fall completely off the wagon and eat whatever I want and not worry about the time or the effort that goes into working out.*

That disturbing journey is where my head takes me when I don't consistently work out and eat right because sitting on my ass doesn't stimulate my body chemistry into releasing those hormones that make it easier for my body to function. They are the same hormones that are associated with a runner's high or sex or sneezing (pepper, anyone?).

I can cite a thousand studies indicating that a balanced eating plan and exercise positively impact your body chemistry and mood and productivity and, let's face it, your overall life experience. I'm not going to waste your time or mine bringing up the studies because you already know that you have to take care of yourself physically.

More than likely, you have some sort of food pattern or habit that you follow, and you've got your "go-to" items and your "cheat" items and your "can't live without" food and beverages. And, at this point, if you're not cool with your current energy level or your physical condition, or if your system is shutting down because it just isn't getting the nutrients it needs to regenerate body cells and keep the wheel greased, then your current eating plan is sabotaging you. And the best part about this realization is that most everybody knows they eat like shit when they're eating like shit. It's typically not some sneaky hidden problem that can't be pinpointed.

But here's the wrinkle and the reason most diets don't work in the long term: The process of feeding yourself is much more than just putting food in your mouth. It becomes symbolic of your self-control, or lack thereof. Eating is the most tangible representation of the control you believe you have in your life. Your eating choices are driven more by psychology than by basic nutritional needs.

So, when you try to do a complete 180 with your eating plan, your Ego starts to freak out a little because you're making a conscious choice that makes no sense to the Ego. Your attempt at improvement is actually throwing your entire system of what you eat and when you eat out of balance, which sends the Ego into an "all hands on deck" status. Like I've said a million times already (enter hyperbole), the Ego does not like change. And when you make such a significant change that impacts your physical, mental, and emotional systems, then you'll pay for it because there will ultimately be some level of backlash for your going so far off route. Most of the time you end up regaining most, if not all, of the weight you lost. Adopting a diet is like trying to take a giant leap into something instead of taking the small steps necessary for your system to adapt and be able to accept a new system as the norm.

Have you ever heard of a scuba diver getting the "bends"? This happens to divers when they go on a deep dive and try to come to the surface too fast. There are gradual changes in a diver's body as he descends into the depths, and the body gets accustomed to the pressure and to the way it processes chemicals to keep itself alive and functioning while at deeper depths. This is the same as your gradual descent into your current eating plan.

Over years and years of eating around your experiences and your lifestyle and your heartbreaks and your coping and your stress and your shitty days and your amazing days, you have found yourself at the bottom of that deep dive, completely accustomed to the pressure. Going on a diet would be like the boat lowering down a rope that you tie around your waist and that boat pulling you up to the surface as quickly as possible, resulting in your not being able to adjust to the drastic change in pressure, leading to a big imbalance in your system and, in certain circumstances, the "bends."

Making such a drastic change in a system that has been

slowly molded into place over years and years is a terrible idea and will end up doing more harm than good. And, since I've been personally dealing with this scenario pretty much my whole life, I can say I tried every type of approach I could think of to keep myself in good physical shape and the only way to the promised land is to . . .

Do it slowly.

I'm trying to think of a personal experience to add in here to make my point, and I can't stop thinking about my "thing" with bread. Seriously, bread is the SHIT! For me, there aren't many things better than fresh baked bread out of the oven or a basket of hot rolls brought out to my table at a restaurant.

If you'd asked me five years ago if I could ever "give up" bread, I would have scoffed at the very notion. But it was about that time I came around to realize that bread, the massive simple carb-delivery devil that it is, is not the best of choices for my system. It's not like I decided to conveniently label myself as a celiac or even the more subtle, slightly more palatable "gluten intolerant"; I just figured out that the way my body chemistry operates, I felt better, more balanced, more energetic, and looked better when I decided to go bread-free. So, at that point, I made the decision to gradually wean my way off bread, seriously thinking that I didn't want to give up such a treat to myself.

You see, my attachment to bread was not only the amazing comforting texture and taste, but the emotional sense that I was giving up or losing something that has brought me much pleasure throughout my life. And I knew that if I went cold turkey, similar to a big shift that starting a diet represents, it wasn't going to happen because, let's face it, we are all that snotty-faced kid deep down inside, and if someone tells us we "can't" have something, we obsess over it. This would result in my being pissed that I am denying myself bread, even though it's my own choice because it's best for me in the long run. And my system, being physically and psychologically used to having some level of bread in my life, would fight such a radical "all of a sudden it's gone" approach.

So, this is what I decided to do (and, for the record, it worked): I started by having only low-carb tortillas in my house but still allowed myself bread when I was out and about. Then, once I did that for a while (I'm talking months), I totally got used to the low-carb tortillas at home and they completely satisfied my carb needs. Then, I started to make some very subtle changes when I was out to eat, like taking the bottom of the bun off my burger or having two hot, cloth-napkin-covered rolls instead of three. I would hold myself to that routine for a few months, while forgiving any backslides that happened (and they totally did) especially during a 2 a.m. end-of-a-bender run to Drunk Denny's. (Moons Over My Hammy with a couple extra pieces of buttered rye . . . hell yeah!)

Getting to the point where I don't miss bread anymore, where I can now get my fix by having a burger or a couple rolls every now and then, took a long-ass time. It was a baby-steps process that allowed my system to gradually acclimate to the new "less bread" environment, similar to the diver who has to rise to the surface slowly after a deep dive. It's all about allowing your entire system to move at the same pace as your goals or having the realization that deep change—change that will stick and become you—happens as part of a process that takes a lot longer than you probably want it to as you're eyeing your reflection in the bathroom mirror thinking you need to get into "beach shape." It will happen, but real results probably won't be seen and felt until next bikini season.

Let's face it, a lot of people do not have the patience for that. I know that once I grasped the slow-and-steady concept and put it to work and actually saw how successful it was, I knew that was the way to go, and that is how you can make it work for you. Plus, seriously, we are all our own worst critic, so put on that bathing suit and own it because, truth be told:

NO ONE ELSE REALLY GIVES TWO SHITS ABOUT HOW YOU LOOK, AND IF THEY DO, REMEMBER, IT'S A THEM THING, NOT A "YOU" THING!

Let's Get Physical . . . Physical

Along with choosing the right food to shove into your pie-hole, it would make perfect sense that it's just as important to respect your body with physical fitness.

Personally, I've been into physical fitness since my high school days, mostly because I grew up with a thing called body dysmorphia. If you're not familiar, it's an Ego program that made me feel like I was a fat tub of goo, even though I wasn't. It all stemmed from my being a "husky" kid, or big-framed and the comments I would hear because of it, especially from people in my own house.

Unfortunately, these comments would be interpreted by me as them calling me fat. And when that happened, especially when it came from a parent, it created a big Ego imprint on my self-image, which I have been dealing with my whole life. Even after going through all the work on myself as I have, I am still prone to slip into that initial thought of not being in the best shape I could be, even though, in the grand scheme of things, I keep myself in good shape.

Now, I have to say at this point, when I'm talking about physical fitness, I'm not just talking about your body shape. I'm talking about everything having to do with respecting your body, which includes making good food choices and exercising for the purpose of gaining some muscle mass and improving your cardiovascular system and balancing your body chemistry, which will help to calm you and balance out your emotional swings. It also means getting adequate sleep.

For the record, my emphasis on physical fitness is not to be in Olympic shape; it's about finding what works for you, like walking, running, lifting weights, yoga, Insanity, P90X, Pilates, naked Zumba—whatever. It's not about looking like anyone else because that's reactionary and not representative of your True Self. It's about tuning up your physical system, moving around, and getting some oxygen flowing. I know personally that this is a very important part of the whole process. And, if you are dealing with or have dealt with body dysmorphia, then I could not be more empathetic. It's a bitch to fight through that sometimes, but once you gain some insight through the steps in this program and get better at pattern interrupting that shitty program, your life will become instantly better because, by accepting your body vessel for what it is—which is not you, but a mere container of your True Self—you will no longer compare yourself to anyone else.

As long as you know that you're putting forth the effort to take care of your body, you can rest assured that your shape and features, warts and all, are just part of the deal, part of you, and your acceptance of that will lead you to letting go of that insecurity and opening up a whole new channel of energy to help you move forward. Because once you accept your physical self, others will as well. But you have to do it first. Remember, the physical part of you is just as important as the mental, emotional, and spiritual parts. The more dialed in your physical system is, the more it releases those good body chemicals, which help you spark those nether regions of your brain, leading to new, expanded thoughts about what the hell you want to do with yourself.

A New Twist on the Vision Board

Another good tool to ground you that tends to reveal good project ideas is the vision board. I'm going to assume you have an idea of what a vision board is. However, just in case you need a refresher, it's when you cut out a bunch of pictures from magazines that illustrate how you want your life to be or what you want to have in your life, and then you glue your pictures to a poster board and hang it somewhere you can see it every day.

Basically, it's a visual representation of you, your Vision, and your Gifts. It's how you envision your "perfect" life, like the things or events that you think will fulfill you. This tool is all about doing a little trickery on the brain, similar to the mantra on the card I talked about earlier. The tool follows the proven notion that if you can visualize it as "already existing," the brain thinks it does exist, and then you create an energy field that acts like a magnet and begins to attract the things that are included on your vision board. (This is the Law of Attraction at work.)

Most of the time when a vision board is created for use in therapy, it's plastered with pictures ranging from a mansion, a yacht, and a mountain chateau with a roaring fireplace and a mounted Yeti head wearing a permanently shocked expression to some d-bag with a roll of tube socks in his trousers leaning against a red Maserati and smiling so large you can fit said roll of socks in his mouth. My natural instinct when I see a vision board littered with this nonsense is to find the culprit responsible and give him a gold star on his forehead so I have something to aim at. However, seeing as though I am able to "quickly" pattern interrupt myself out of my natural inclination to bitch-slap idiots, I instead start to see this kind of vision board for what it is: a cry for help.

Superficial goals like these are centered on "things" and not expansion. The material goals like a big house or a yacht or exotic car are empty goals; they mean nothing in the grand scheme of things if you attain them without grounding yourself in what being fulfilled really is. And I can tell you, being fulfilled does not come from owning crap because material objects cannot—I repeat, cannot—bring anyone fulfillment.

It's the whole story about Gordon Gekko in the 1987 film *Wall Street*. (For you youngsters, this was a kickass movie with Charlie Sheen before he went "Winning!" and with Michael Douglas when he was just slightly old.) In the movie, Gordon played by Douglas is this big-time Wall Street dude with mega-bucks, and his protégé, Bud, played by a relatively sober Sheen, confronts him about how much is enough. The specific scene I want to bring up goes like this:

Bud asks, "Tell me, Gordon, when does it all end?

How many yachts can you water ski behind? How much is enough?"

And, of course, Gekko twists his answer into not being a question of being enough, but of it all being a game. Why? Because Gordon's fulfillment comes in playing the game and screwing over other people and being in competition and winning, and not in the "stuff" that he has attained because:

NO TRUE FULFILLMENT CAN BE OBTAINED BY ACQUIRING MATERIAL OBJECTS.

So, that being said, you've come this far, so don't start down the wrong path by cutting out a bunch of pictures from *Rich Douchebag Illustrated* or *Gold-Diggers Magazine.* Instead, find pictures and symbols that represent where you want to be with your soul, with your spirit, with your Purpose. I'm talking about pictures like that guy who stops his car in the middle of the road, gets out, and helps the old lady across the street, or a photo of a mom in a flowing sundress walking her three-year-old daughter along the beach during sunset, or a pic of an artist working on a beautiful abstract painting using only partially melted Chinese crayons and a travel-size bottle of hand sanitizer.

Fill up your vision board with images of how your life would look if you dialed yourself in to your True Self and started to manifest your life in the Big World the way you've always wanted, hopefully with love and joy and cool experiences and people you care about and service and success and expansion. I'm not saying you can't have your yacht or cars or your roll of tube socks because the act of putting yourself on the path of fulfillment will also bring you money and things. But instead of those things being the goal, they are actually a "result" or a byproduct of your fulfillment and of your being on the path you're supposed to travel.

And the weird thing is, when you get to the point where your success starts to blossom and the money starts showing up and you have the ability to buy more stuff if you want, that stuff won't matter so much to you because by that time, you will have schooled yourself on what fulfillment really is.

By making this board and putting it to good use, you are essentially setting yourself up for success by creating an energy around you called *creative tension*. What I mean by that is the board sets a clear distinction between where you are now and where you want to go. And, in doing so, you have created a tension between the two points that will actually pull you toward your goals.

It's like there's a rubber band stretched between where you are now and where you want to be. The tension will manifest itself in your being more open, consciously and subconsciously, to opportunities that come your way that will lead you to your goals. And, in the case of our baby-steps exercise, the tension will help you open up your mind to your passions and interests and different ideas on what first steps you would like to take.

Oh, before I leave this one, I have to add that the same rule applies with the board as with the mantra card. Once you start to feel the impact of the board lessening, or the second you catch yourself with any sense of doubt after looking at the board, then turn that sucker around. You'll be able to turn it back around once something happens in your life that gives you back a little more sense of hope and confidence. Go ahead and add new pictures or make a new board if you feel as though the old board doesn't speak to you. The more you expand, the higher the chance that your awareness will shift, which might lead to new visions of fulfillment.

Dear Diary

Along with the vision board, I am a true believer in the power of journaling to free your creative mind to bring about some great project ideas.

Have you ever heard of a creative block? This is a thing that artists deal with when their creative juice river suddenly runs dry for no apparent reason. If you've never experienced this phenomenon, I just have to say, it's insanely frustrating. Invariably, the block typically comes at a time when an artist needs the creative flow the most, which is actually the reason the block shows up—too much pressure. So, even though I'm bringing this up as an artist's frustration, it's actually a condition most of us have encountered.

Which leads me to sharing a terrific solution. There's an iconic book called *The Artists Way*, and it's brilliant. It really helped me to get out of a creative funk I was in a little while ago. The book shares some tools and techniques to get one's creative flow back on track. For me, the most important tool I took away from that book was journaling.

The author, Julia Cameron, famously calls journaling the Morning Papers, which sounds like it has to do with dropping your Sunday morning deuce while thumbing through pointless BuzzFeed articles, all the while being constantly aware that one false move and your smartphone is swimmin' with the kids. So, I like to keep it simple and just refer to it as *journaling*.

The process involves journaling three full pages every morning of whatever comes to mind. This exercise provides two very important grounding tools. First, it allows you to just write, and you're not writing a typical diary entry. The journal is essentially a stream of consciousness because when you sit down and just start to write, more than likely you'll scribble down a bunch of nonsense at first because your conscious brain is feeling pressure to write something and it really isn't having fun with an exercise that directs you to write down stuff that doesn't make any sense. But if you keep writing, while at the same time stopping the editing in your head, you'll find by about a page and half in you are freed up to allow your True Self to start speaking through the pen. It will be one of those surreal feelings, like you are detached from your hand and you don't have any idea what will be written next, the flow bypassing your controlling cognitive brain and expressing some very deep thoughts and feelings. And with this free-flow dump comes a lot of interesting stuff. You'll be surprised at what comes out when you zone out and just let your hand write stuff.

After the three pages are done, you really don't even have to look back at what you've written because the sole act of writing it down has brought a number of things to the surface, some being True Self goals and others being Ego-based fears that you may not have known existed or now know where they may have come from. The act of writing actually purges the mind and acts as a solid grounding mechanism, stemming from the newfound knowledge you have about yourself, which we refer to simply as awareness.

The second big benefit of journaling is the fact that it is a meditative experience. Even though you aren't sitting crisscross applesauce with eyes closed and chanting some mantra, you are still putting your mind in a calm and controlled space where you are able to tap into your Inner Self.

Most of the time, I don't go back and read my pages because the point of writing is not to document stuff; it's more of a venting situation. However, sometimes I find myself writing something that's a bit of a mind-blower, or a huge light-bulb-turns-on-over-the-head epiphany, and I know that breakthrough needs to be remembered. In that case, I use the top of the page and the area along the left side of the page to jot down my special "must remember" notations. That way, I can do a month's worth of journaling and be able to go back through the pages and easily find the really important stuff.

Personally, the process of journaling has done more to open up my mind to project ideas and first steps than any other tool. It's almost like opening up the floodgates of your mind, and out of the flow comes a ton of creative ideas.

Make Your Own Top-10 List

This one is pretty cut and dry and very easy to do. But I have to admit, I was never one to make a daily "to-do" list. No particular conscious reason, it just wasn't my thing. But once I made the decision to expand my life with my coaching business and consistently produce the podcast and shoot videos, and especially write this book, I knew I would need a little help in the focus and organization department. So it just made sense to grab a notepad every night and scribble down the things I wanted to work on the next day. It has helped keep me on track and focused, although I struggled at the beginning with prioritizing the things I wanted to do. So, I sort of modified how I made my list, and it has really helped.

Here's what works for me:

First and foremost—and this is very important—if you have one grand goal, you've got to list it at the top of the page every day. What I mean by "grand" is the big goal you have in mind that won't necessarily be completed by day's end but will be accomplished by you making baby steps every day. For instance, my grand goal over the past few months was to complete this book. Of course, there are a lot of steps involved in this endeavor, but by listing the big one at the top, it kept me focused on the need to make small, incremental daily steps toward completion. And, for the record, this approach is actually validated by research about how effective these lists are with productivity. Just take a look at the very popular book *Getting Things Done* by David Allen. This book, along with supporting research, has spawned an almost cultish following that is known as the Getting Things Done (GTD) Philosophy.

However, what if you don't have a grand goal? You may not, and that is perfectly fine. Through your everyday exploration into stuff that interests you, the to-do list can be a very effective tool for uncovering a more concrete goal.

One quick tip regarding the wording of your "to-dos": Make them action-oriented and specific. For instance, if you need to write a report, then put "type out report, spell check, and submit," instead of just "report" or "finish report." This way, your subconscious is getting a very clear action directive that will create internal momentum to getting it done.

When it comes to planning, I really need to keep it simple, or I'll lose interest and just try to wing it, which typically doesn't help get things done. So, I break my list up into basic sections:

- The work stuff

- The have-tos

- The errands

- The project

- The fun stuff

The work stuff is pretty self-explanatory. The have-tos are things like going to the dentist or calling your mom for her birthday. Then there are the errands. From food shopping to dry cleaning to picking up an anniversary card, these are the timely things that, if we don't do them, will bite us in the ass. After all, starvation, dirty laundry with hovering stink clouds like Pigpen's, and a girlfriend's wrath can be real buzz kills.

Then comes the to-do list for the project, which is a list that entails how you will give time to your interests and passions and developing the part of your life that will allow you to best share your Gift with the world. For me, my project to-do list encompasses the things I need to do to complete this book, like conducting research, doing competitive analyses, talking to clients, and hiring an editor.

Finally comes the to-do list for fun stuff. Although I don't want you to think fun should only come after everything else or that the things on a project or even work to-do lists aren't fun themselves. The fun to-do list is more about remembering to take self-care time and check off the list the things we can do to decompress, recharge, and practice some of the things discussed in this book, like grabbing a nap, going for a run, meditating, journaling, or taking in dinner and a nice glass of Franzia Estate Reserve from a newly opened box.

I know that when you sit down and scribble out a list like this, there will most likely be a lot of things on there to the point where you think there is no way you're going to get to all of them. That being said, here's the rub: Having your stuff written out in front of you gives you a great opportunity to maybe rethink the way you've set up your life.

If your lists, day after day, are mostly work and have-tos and errands, you'll never have the space to treat yourself to a little fun or to put effort into feeding your passion and expanding your fulfillment through a project. And, even after taking a look at the list and reprioritizing a little, there will still be some days where you just won't be able to get to all the stuff you want to, especially if some wild card event happens.

That's cool because some days will not go as planned, which doesn't matter in the grand scheme of things. Plans are general guidelines that are supposed to keep you focused on the things you want to accomplish in your life. I know a Monday list will look a hell of a lot different than a Saturday list. My point is to use your lists to incorporate some balance in your life. When you take a look at a week's worth of lists or even a month's worth, assess whether there is a good flow and if there is as much cheat time as there is crunch time allotted.

Reminder: Don't be a martyr; it's no fun, it's not attractive, and nobody cares.

Bottom Line: Your to-do lists are not about getting

to everything on them. They're about documenting what you believe serves you and acts as a reminder of how you choose to spend your precious time. You will not find your bliss or increase your level of fulfillment unless you create space for your project and for some fun.

Inner and Outer Support Systems

In the process of making the world your bitch, you will find there are two kinds of support systems you can create that will prop you up when you need a little compassionate understanding or kick you in the butt when you think about giving up. First, there is inner support. I'm talking about that inner feeling or sense of empowerment; basically, I'm talking about your level of *confidence*.

I'm talking about that voice in your head that tells you to "Get the fuck up!" when you fall, and "You got this!" and "Everything happens for a reason," along with all the other words of encouragement and faith you have in yourself.

What I'm *not* talking about is that dick of an Ego that likes to put on that hastily crafted True Self mask and try to fool you into believing its voice is really you or what you believe or what you want. "I'm not good enough. I'm an idiot. I can't do this," are the Ego whispers that haunt you. "I'm not good-looking enough. I failed again . . . what a loser. Why would anyone want to be with me?"

Dialing in on the true inner voice of support creates a solid and consistent Foundation within yourself so you can effectively weather the storms, inside and outside, that come your way. Instead of breaking out the shame and disappointment whip, you can quickly shift into your more aware and present True Self channel, which leads to shifting your perspective from an Ego-defined "failure" to a True Self defined, "Hmm, that did not turn out as planned, but what can I learn from this bump in the road?"

Then there is your outer support, which is your family, your friends, maybe a coworker, a therapist, or even a support group. Regarding your outer support, even the closest friend you have right now or your closest family relationship may not cut the mustard when it comes to supporting you, especially right now because you are in the midst of big-time expansion and growth and a lot of people may have a hard time with that.

The person or persons in your support circle must have the ability and willingness to get you and be there for you in a way that works for you and, at the same time, isn't so far out of their range that they start to feel as though being your supporter at that level is too much for them to handle. Because when that happens, get ready for the old passive-aggressive behavior patterns, like they're starting not to answer texts in their normal time window or not being "available" to chat or suddenly finding excuses not to hang out. Basically, their Ego's fear of losing themselves translates into them backing away from your life. It's not that they are bad or uncaring people, it's just that they feel as though you need more from them than their personal protection boundaries will allow.

As you go through your expansion and become a "different" person now, which is really just your True Self, you stop identifying with your Ego programs and align more with your True Self. This results in a change in you on all levels—mental, emotional, physical, and spiritual.

The channeled positive energy can literally be seen in a glow, like when you suspect a woman is pregnant or someone is in love or when someone got a little somethin'-somethin' the night before. You start to radiate, and people notice. Most people will not be able to put a finger on the difference, but they will have this feeling that something is different about you. And the cool part about it is, the positive energy acts like a magnet and is contagious. This change may even go so far as to expose the fact that your current relationship (girlfriend, boyfriend, hubby, wife, Japanese body pillow) may not be a good fit for your inner circle.

This happens quite a bit, due to the fact that the Ego-driven you had a "need" for something that particular person brought to the table. And now that you are expanding out of that shitty Ego stuff and are able to be much more aware and clear about what works and what doesn't work for you, two things will start to happen:

1. You will first begin to notice other people's . . . let's just say "lack of enthusiasm" when it comes to your new-found discoveries about yourself or your shift in how you see and conduct your life now. Their lack of enthusiasm will then, clearly, not sit well with you, which will then turn into the realization that you now see your relationship with that person in a whole new light.

2. Then, these so-called support people will begin to notice your shift, which, to them, seems like you are turning into a different person, which will then lead to a "fear" trigger in them because they will think that you are leaving them behind. Or you're just such a different person now that your former support people can't relate to you like they used to, meaning you're no longer just treading water like they are, which subconsciously to them

means abandonment or rejection. Yikes! No wonder so many people are scared shitless of change because with change comes CHANGE!

The Ego hates change—hates it—because any change holds a component of unknown, which could lead to elevated risk, which could lead to death, which is what the Ego thinks is happening and is trying to prevent. That is why most people get to a point where they believe they are where they are supposed to be, mostly because of what their parent or parents drilled into their mind about their worth to the world, which sets a limit on personal empowerment and confidence. Then they settle, they find that groove, and then they look around to make sure they are keeping up appearances to convince the neighbors and themselves that they are doing good, which leads to unfulfilled dreams and an unsatisfactory life, emptiness, and loneliness, even when surrounded by their "loved ones," and depression and guilt.

Take a quick look yourself, and I bet this scenario is playing out with others around you. Because we are surrounded by people who don't like their lives or are trying to talk themselves into liking their lives by rationalizing that they haven't sold out, when the real story is they are either too ignorant or too scared to go after what they really want.

That's why the concept of "keeping up with the Joneses" is so prevalent. All you have to do is find your groove, like being married with 2.3 kids, living in a middle-class suburban neighborhood, cutting your lawn with an environmentally friendly solar-powered push mower, and driving your late-model soccer mom van with the purple-drink-stained left rear seat, all while keeping one eye on your checking account balance and the other eye on your neighbors and what cars they are driving and what clothes they are wearing and what highly Yelp-rated public charter school they are trying to get their spoiled brat into and what store they shop at. . . . blah, blah, blah, you get the picture.

It depressed me just to write that, and, I'm hoping it gave you an uneasy feeling as well, or, let's be honest, if you're cool with that vision of life, you'd be better off depositing this book in a family-sized compost bin (made from the most durable nonrecyclable polymers), firing up the old laptop, and starting to binge-buy decorative bath soaps on Etsy.

Bottom line is, both your inner support and your outer support will change as you go through your journey. And there's a very good chance this will create a lot of turmoil in your life. But that is actually good because the process of change exposes the hidden problems you're trying to figure out in the first place, like the problems with your thinking patterns and the people in your life that you believed supported you but didn't or who really can't, now that you've decided to grow and they haven't.

The key is to surround yourself with your tribe, good people who will support your journey. If you don't have people like this in your life, I suggest you look for them or put yourself out in the world in such a way that supporters can find you. It's about using your energy to attract like-minded people who operate on the same frequency as you. This isn't about finding a bunch of head-bobbing sycophants who think exactly the same way or agree on everything; it's about finding those people who support you for who you are, who at the same time are still able to continue to be themselves and have their own opinions. They aren't caught up in their negative Ego patterns to be threatened by your dance with your True Self. To the proper supporters, being around you is not anything like death—it is life itself!

To find other like-minded people, put yourself in situations where you share the same interests and/or passions with others. For instance, volunteer with an organization you feel strongly about, or take a class based on something that fires you up, like cooking or photography or improv. Tell everyone you can about your journey and see who seems genuinely interested.

Those who give off an ever-so-subtle sign of "WTF?" will surely make their level of "support capability" known by turning glassy-eyed as they attempt to stay with your conversation, or, my personal favorite, when they throw out a follow-up question that involves some level of confusion and biting judgment, something like, "Wow, that's great, but why would you do something like that?" or "Wow, good luck with that."

Next, try the Internet. The World Wide Web of carnal delights is by far the best free and effortless way to get yourself and your message out to anyone who will listen or read or watch. I'm not saying you have to start creating viral videos featuring you and your gender-neutral cat, Dakota, braiding each other's hair, or that you have to start a weekly blog defending inappropriate human/animal relationships, or that you should invest a bunch of money in creating some elaborate website, or to buy Google ads to promote said relationship. I'm saying, take your current interest or interests (they don't even have to be passions at this point) and start your search for other people who share your interest. And the best part about the Internet is, there is so much unique, creative, weird, funky, disturbing, random shit out there, you are bound to find at least a couple of people (or at least a compassionate spambot) you can relate to and begin to communicate with about shared thoughts or experiences.

The Trick to Creating an Effective Plan

The primary purpose of a plan or a long-term goal should be to provide a guideline that allows for a lot of room to experiment and improvise, and fall down, and get back up and keep experimenting!

I think very specific goals do way more harm than good.

Let's say your ultimate or long-term goal is to become a famous singer. First of all, wanting to be "famous" is an Ego thing—no way around that—all Ego! So, you're already starting off on the wrong foot. A much better way to phrase this goal, or as I like to call it, the True Self version of the goal, would be, "I will commit and work hard every day to develop my singing Gift and share it with the world to my fullest potential in whatever situation the universe creates for me."

When it's phrased like that, you take it out of the "comparing me to famous people" zone and turn it into your own, genuine life journey statement. When you do it that way, you commit to learning and growing in your own flow and you own your own Gift, in whatever way it develops (no comparing to other people). You surrender to the universal flow, which basically means you open yourself up to the opportunities that present themselves to you.

In this case, it could be where you do an open mic at a local coffee shop and some game creator hears you and wants you to do voice-over and sing a couple songs for the next Grand Theft Auto knockoff release. And then, as you are recording on some dingy soundstage, you meet up with some small-time producer who is looking for a vocalist for a new band he's creating, which leads to Tuesday night gigs in some dive bar.

You are having a great time and you continue to be grateful and hone your vocal Gift until the bench coach from the local double-A baseball team wanders into the bar because he just caught his wife with the team mascot, and in between shots of Mezcal and Grape Fanta, he hears you and wants to bring you in to sing the National Anthem during the next home stand. And then the Major League team's traveling secretary hears your great rendition and asks you to fly to New York and sing on opening day, and so on, and so on . . .

And all the while, you are having the time of your life, completely fulfilled, doing what you love and finding ways to share your Gift with the world. Do you see what I'm trying to point out here?

Following a plan based on your True Self will get the wheels moving much faster and in the direction you're supposed to go, versus acting on an Ego-motivated goal or plan that will end up leading you off your path and into a lot of dead ends until you wise up and tap into your True Self.

So, if you have a specific picture in your mind of reaching a huge goal, ask yourself, honestly, "Why do I want this specific goal?"

The answer may surprise you because a lot of our goal setting has more to do with unresolved Ego issues than it does with our putting the time and effort into knowing ourselves, discovering our Gift, and creating a plan to share that Gift with the rest of the world.

If you listen closely enough, you're bound to hear a lot of:

"I want to be famous."

"I want to be rich."

"I want to be important."

These statements are like putting the cart before the horse because you can't "be" any of those things; you can only "be" who you are. When you do go through the steps to discover who you are underneath all that skin and bones and other mush, then you will realize *the ultimate goal is to "be" YOU.*

Because when you tap into that flow of Universal energy, you'll find the simple act of figuring out who the hell you are will bring about the fame, the riches, and the importance you seek in your Ego mind, but in a more pure, True Self way, which turns out like this:

1. You will "attract" the people into your life you are supposed to have around you for your growth, and you will help them learn and grow at the same time (i.e., you will be famous and important).

2. You will manifest or create the amount of money necessary for you to live and thrive in the natural state of your True Self (i.e., you will be *rich*).

A weird thing happens when you decide to get real with yourself and stop listening to all the Ego bullshit and stop comparing your life to other people's: The necessity you once had to think that "everyone" knows who you are or that "everyone" thinks you are important or that you have a ton of scratch in the bank all goes away—*poof!* Because all that shit is not you to begin with; it's what you thought you needed to be for you to feel like you had worth or power in the world.

Take a look at instances of people who do become famous or get really rich or rise to the ranks of importance, and notice how many of those success stories unravel. What's happening is once they've achieved their specific ultimate goal, these Ego-driven people immediately start to sabotage themselves. You know, like Bernie Madoff and the Wall Street Ponzi scheme, or Jared Fogle the Subway guy with the child porn, or Britney Spears's breakdown a few years back, or Bill Cosby and his spiked pudding pops, or the Bieber meltdowns, or the rich and famous people who overdosed or killed themselves. This has to do with their goal of rich and famous being Ego-driven and, ultimately, unfulfilling because their goals didn't represent their True Self. The act of becoming rich and famous didn't get any of these people closer to learning to "be" who they are.

Nothing exists in the Big World (all the stuff and people and events that exists outside of yourself) that can fulfill your True Self—NOTHING!

You've reached this point in our journey together with a better understanding of what does fulfill you and can now sit down in a quiet corner with some form of delicious beverage and/or snack (Tip: Stay away from the off-brand Mexican "cheetos"), and get real with yourself when answering the question, "What Gift do I have that I will commit and work hard every day to develop and share with the world to my fullest potential, in whatever situation the universe creates for me?"

That being said, I want to circle back to the downfall of having a specific goal scenario. In that "famous singer" example I used a couple of pages back, you might envision yourself on stage at the Grammy Awards, holding your trophy in your left hand and fighting off Kanye West with a WWE-style right arm shiver as you attempt to give your acceptance speech, making sure to mention all of the "little" people who you've stepped on along the way. (For the record, I have zero problem with having a goal like that.) Well done!

But, here's what happens. In the process of setting your end point—in this case, being on stage accepting your accolade—you are creating a very specific definition of what success looks like to you. And, in doing so, you set yourself up for a lot of unnecessary pain and disappointment because in visualizing a very specific goal, you will make decisions along the way that you believe will lead you in the most direct path to that specific goal. This creates a problem because you will force certain decisions instead of trusting your natural flow. And when you are in a place where you think you know more than the Universe, you automatically give the Ego big-time power in critiquing your every little move if all of your choices don't lead directly to your specific goal.

The act of being very specific with your goal results in a good chance you will make decisions that are influenced by the Ego (like thinking that moving to New York and studying with Taylor Swift's very expensive vocal coach is the "best" way you can get a leg up on the "competition" and be "better" and "stand out"). Now, I'm sure that particular move would have some benefits, but the point is, it may be WAY out of your flow because it may put you and/or your family in a tough financial position, displacing you out of town and away from solid, supportive relationships or even taking you away from serendipitously running into your natural flow moment.

A natural flow moment would be something like hanging where you are for the time being and making connections through some around-town gigs, which leads you to meet some local producer who will get you set up with an amazing vocal coach who really brings out your talent as a local standout. This, in turn, can get you some serious publicity in your town, where some connected person sees you and pitches your talents to Taylor Swift's management team, which leads to great singing experiences in your life, quite possibly leading to a Grammy.

Let's be honest, there are a lot of amazing singers out there who didn't completely rearrange their lives and were able to bloom into the best singers they were capable of being, sharing their unique Gift with all of us. ("Friday" loves you, Rebecca Black.)

This hyperfocus and Ego-generated belief that there is only one way to get to where you want to go is absolutely, positively not authentic to your flow, to your True Self. The result is that you create a lot of inner tension because you are setting yourself up in a very black-and-white situation where your inner dialogue may end up being something like, "If I don't reach that goal, then I have failed," or "I'm a failure."

This is a *very* tricky situation to navigate, especially

because most successful people tout the benefits of having goals and the benefits of imagery (like running that movie in your mind of how you want things to turn out). And, for the record, I have no problem with any of that, but there is one very important thing you must know and own in creating a plan and venturing forth on your journey: For the plan to work how it's supposed to and ultimately lead you along your path to full expansion and fulfillment, you just have to revise your goal statement to read something like this:

"I will **commit** and **work hard** to develop my Gift and share it with the world to my fullest potential."

Balance Your Own Way

I know this guy who owned a very successful business, was married, and had two kids. He was one of those guys who found his passion and created a kick-ass business around it. Most of his time was put into his business, even though he had his family and friends in the mix. But you know something? Even though that guy spent most of his time with his business, he did a brilliant job at balancing his focus and attention toward the other important parts of his life.

His wife had no issues, his kids were very well adjusted with a strong relationship with their dad, and he had a small but close group of friends who would do anything for him. Everyone understood what balance was to this guy, and it had zero to do with how much time he allocated to the different parts of his life. Balance had everything to do with the quality of time and the depth of presence he gave.

So, at this point, when you lay your life out on the table, how balanced does it look? What small tweaks can you make to create more of a balance? Try using the aforementioned to-do list exercise to possibly expose where your energy is currently going versus where you want it to go in order to create more balance in your life.

Experiment, Prototype, Improvisation

Remember, it's not about "everyone" being open to your Gift; it's a matter of first molding your Gift to speak to a group of people who share a good amount of your foundational beliefs and that you think would be more open to your Gift project than others.

Seth Godin, one of my favorite thinkers, authors, and speakers, calls this "finding your tribe." Start small with your experimenting. That way you can be more flexible in order to see if your Vision action plan is being understood by others the way you want. The prototyping means creating whatever you need to help the Big World understand. There is a chance you may have to invent something or establish a unique way to explain your Gift. And what are the best possible prototype techniques to try? Story-telling and using analogies, of course.

The Incredible Power of the Story

We humans have a thing for stories. They come across as pleasant or entertaining, they generate emotion, and they connect the left and right hemispheres of the brain, all resulting in your message being understandable and remembered. Using analogies allows your specific audience to relate to the message, internalize it, and process it.

For instance, if you're trying to get a point across to a small group of mechanics, your story will be full of analogies about cars and parts and traffic and grease and monkeys, and so on. So you prototype your message, carefully going over it and honing it into the masterpiece you know that it is. Then you confidently deliver your message, only to find out that some of your points seemed to stick while others seemed to be invisible or, even worse, steered the audience in the wrong direction (you just have to go with an accidental pun like that). At this point, it's now time to start to adjust, or improvise.

The *improvisation* part has to do with being flexible, in making small adjustments as you go. I 100-percent guarantee that your original Vision will have to be tweaked in one way or another as you go through the process of finding out how to most effectively communicate your message because everybody has to make adjustments.

Maintenance and Adjustments

One of the best pieces of advice I ever got was from one of my first bosses. On my first day at the office, he took me aside and said, "Son, the key to being successful is living your life like an Olympic gymnast. Wear something tight, force a smile, lie about your age, and be flexible."

This has to do with not only being flexible but also with being a realist, accepting the fact that you will definitely trip and fall along the way. If you don't, then you're not taking big enough steps or you are delusional. And when you trip, the key is to get the hell up, brush yourself off, and figure out what adjustments need to be made in order to continue on your path of expansion and kick-assery.

The necessity of making an adjustment is based on the assumption that your trip and fall were the result of reaching for something you have not attained before or from stepping out of your comfort zone. Basically, the result of the previously mentioned steps of experimenting, proto-typing, and improvising.

That being said, be very careful of the Ego rearing its ugly mug and subconsciously getting you to make the same mistake twice, or three or four or a hundred times. If you make the same mistake a second time, you, my friend, are under Ego control because there is NO WAY you should be making the exact same mistake if you were consciously open to the reasons why you made that particular mistake in the first place.

It's like, let's say, you go in for a job interview and you end up being late and missing your appointment. Now, assuming you weren't dealing with a family emergency or something else that would clearly be more important than the interview, your lateness would be considered a mistake. And whatever the boneheaded maneuver was (not setting your alarm, not anticipating traffic, taking too long to pick out the perfect outfit), if you make yourself late on a dif-ferent occasion because you're waiting for your Spiderman Underoos to come out of the dryer, then you are not only a moron, but your Ego is successfully sabotaging you by diverting your attention.

If that happens, freeze! (Remember the freeze section of this book?) Sit down in your quiet happy place corner and get honest with yourself about what happened that got you to make the same mistake twice. You'll then be able to see the pattern and make the necessary adjustment. And, in this particular case, the pattern was making you late to keep the opportunity of a better job off the table because maybe your Ego was scared of change or that you wouldn't be able to handle the responsibilities of the new job or it didn't want you to succeed so it could keep you safe in your already existing bubble of reality—all sucky reasons, brought to you by the Ego.

Make sure you give yourself time and space to figure your shit out if you are making the same mistake more than once. It's the constant awareness of needed maintenance and adjustments that is really one of the most important steps in your journey.

Failure Doesn't Even Really Exist

As you begin to put legs underneath your plan and you start taking action by experimenting, prototyping, and improvising, there will be some things that work and some things that don't. In fact, you may actually think you've just nailed something and your project will have a huge impact, but when you put it into motion, it flops like an overpaid NBA player. In this circumstance, there's a word that is often used, a word that will do more to halt your progress than any other at this point. Of course, I'm talking about the word *failure*.

I have two takes on this word:

1. In your Inner World, this word actually DOES NOT EXIST. If you are aligned to your True Self and Purpose, with a clear understanding of your Gift, any unsuccessful attempts as you experiment are nothing more than just necessary steps that needed to happen for you to learn and to make corrections or adjustments. The word *failure* has no meaning.

2. In the Big World, failure is a good thing as long as you are on the path to your Purpose. When some idiot points out

that you have failed at something, or worse, that you are a failure, you don't buy it; it doesn't stick. Now, depending on the people and how close they are to you, the comment may sting initially, but with your empowered understanding about the importance and need of adjustments, your initial knee-jerk reaction of getting down on yourself will quickly melt away into the conscious understanding and confidence you have about yourself and the choices you are making along your journey. It's just a damn shame that weak people don't want anyone succeeding around them because it exposes them for the lazy assholes they are, as well as providing a reminder to themselves that they don't have the sack to even try, whereas you are showing the world that you have the confidence of trusting that any setbacks along the way will ultimately lead you to CRUSHING IT!

If you know you are on your path, then anyone using the "F" word toward you or your actions is just a poor soul who doesn't get it. So, have pity while thanking them for reinforcing the fact you are MAKING THINGS HAPPEN. Basically, have your "Look at me now, bitch!" locked and loaded.

Ch-Ch-Ch-Ch-Changes

> "Be easy on yourself. Have fun. Only hang around people that are positive and make you feel good. Anybody who doesn't make you feel good, kick them to the curb. And the earlier you start in your life, the better."
>
> —AMY POEHLER

This is almost a word of warning . . . wait a second, it is a legit paragraph of warning!

As you learn and grow and expand, there will inevitably be both good and bad consequences to your growth. Good consequences would be like discovering an inner excitement, riding a high of newfound energy, and attracting the right people to your life and being able to see growth opportunities when they enter your line of sight.

But what you may not know is that along with all of the good that comes from expansion, there is an equal and opposite force that shows up to the party, which consists of stuff like losing some relationships or falling on your ass more or your life becoming more complicated or more difficult in certain circumstances. This is known as the Unity of Opposites, or yin and yang. I like to use an example of looking through a toilet paper roll, which would limit your view to a pretty small area. One day you realize that you've been holding a crusty old toilet paper roll up to your eye and you pull it away only to find that your view has completely expanded, to the left, to the right, and up and down.

As you grow and expand, you will become more aware and will "see" way more than you have ever seen in your life. This could prove to be both enlightening and overwhelming because when you expand to the "good," you also expand to the "bad." And I'm not saying *bad* in the traditional sense. What I'm saying is that your joys will be higher but your disappointments will be lower, or they could be.

I'm not going to sugarcoat this because I think it's important I give you a heads-up that your decision to expand will create some messes that you'll have to clean up. This concept is just like having a kid, in that it's insanely rich and fulfilling, and at the same time one of the hardest fucking things you'll ever do in your life. So, there's a really good chance that not everyone around you will be okay with your expansion.

There is a great story I like to call the Crab Theory that explains this process very well.

The Crab Theory

It is widely known in the crab fishing world that when you go fishing for one crab, you need to bring a secure container, maybe a bucket with a wire mesh top, because if you just put that one crab in a regular bucket, he'll scurry up, out, and back into the briny deep. However, if you want to catch more than one crab, you need only a regular bucket with no wire mesh top.

Why? Because if one crab tries to climb out of a bucket full of crabs, the others will pull it back in . . . *every time.*

This doesn't happen sometimes; it happens all of the time. And, of course, the analogy is:

Any time other people see you trying to climb up or out to better yourself, there will be some who are going to go to great lengths to pull you back into the bucket.

To these people in your life, you represent progress and, most important, you are pointing out to them that they are stagnant and doing nothing to better themselves. A lot of times, the same person or people who were on your back to make some changes in the first place will be the ones to try to pull you back in. Yeah, very bizarre. This could be your significant other, good friends, any family member, coworker, or even your boss. And the kicker is, your improvement might not have any direct connection to the person. For example, say you've decided to work out again and are now making a couple trips to the gym during the week. Interestingly enough, this might rub your room-mate the wrong way, even though it has nothing directly to do with your job.

Why you ask? Very simple . . .

YOU ARE DOING SOMETHING WITH YOUR LIFE. THEY ARE NOT.

Even a Very Large Baby Takes Baby Steps

Do you remember the story I told you about that seminar I went to that led me to drop an atomic bomb on my life and ended up losing my house, quite a few friends, and all the fun toys I had at the time, and also damaged my rela-tionships with most of my family members?

Well, the lesson I learned from this and would like to share is, when you drop an atomic bomb, there's a LOT of collateral damage, damage that happens to the parts of your life that need to stay intact as you go through your expansion process. I always refer to it like you've been building this foundation or platform your whole life with your choices and the people you brought into your life and your living situation, you know, your life as it is right now. And when you blow up that platform, which is the *only* reality you've been standing on your whole life, freefall time happens. And what's waiting for you at the end of the fall? Probably not a plate of chicken wings and a beer.

This is what I did to myself. I blew everything up and had nothing to hold on to and ended up losing myself. I had nothing solid to stand on while I attempted to make tweaks to my life to get it to where I wanted it to go. Clearly, the moral of the story is "baby steps, small changes."

I have to say, in all seriousness, your newfound knowledge and awareness and the understanding that you are the architect of your own life and there is a legit exit strategy to elevate yourself above the idiots will most definitely act as an energy boost, and you are definitely going to want to reach for Thor's hammer and start fuckin' some shit up.

This is why just listening to a motivational speaker could do more harm than good. You could get all juiced up to go do something, but you don't know what or how to do it. So, I'm saying, back away from the big hammer and pick up a small rock hammer so you can first work on chipping away at the rough outer edges.

An important question that comes up at this point is, "Where do I start?" The answer is pretty simple. If you get into a quiet spot and think about the different things in your life that, by now, you know don't help you to point all of your arrows in the same direction, you can start to see the things that fall along the edges that you know you could more easily chip away. It's at this point that you can break out some of your newfound tools like mindfulness meditation, journaling, and breathing techniques.

There is a natural hierarchy that falls into place when you think about your life and how much more important some things are than other things. I'm thinking that through your process of discovery and awareness and personal empowerment, there has been sort of a running list of things you know should be changed or at least slightly adjusted. So, again, get in that quiet thinking corner and start to jot down those things, people, and situations in your current life that need to be shifted. When you have the list, it becomes pretty clear what the relatively easy adjustments are and what the biggies are. The small adjustment or quick-fix thing on the list that you think is the easiest will be your first project.

For example, instead of quitting my job and breaking off contact with my family of "crabs," I should have looked at making smaller adjustments, such as selling off one of my toys or bouncing some ideas off a friend about how to communicate better with my family. That way, I wouldn't have ended up broke, losing my house, and without any immediate family support.

 **VIDEO TIME: VIDEO #12**

CHAPTER 11

Are You Ready to Change?

"If there is no struggle, there is no progress."

—FREDERICK DOUGLASS

EVEN AFTER ALL WE HAVE BEEN THROUGH up to now, there is still a chance that you may be willing, but not yet capable of making any changes. So, before we go any further, we need to get an idea of how ready you are.

Personally, I don't buy into the basic assumption of most traditional behavioral change models that anyone with the intention to change can make a change. Based on my own experiences and solid research, I believe a person must go through some preliminary steps before they can set themselves up for an effective and lasting change.

There's a supported theory called the transtheoretical model of behavior change. Known as TTM and developed by Prochaska and DiClemente in the late 1970s, this model identifies five distinct stages of change that people move through when modifying behavior. Prochaska and DiClemente's extensive research has determined that less than 20 percent of a population at risk (in need of change) is prepared to take action at any given time. So there's a chance that the reason you haven't been able to get into "action" mode and make a change is because you aren't in a supported "stage" of decision-making. I wouldn't want you to get all bummed out when you continue through this book and can't seem to follow through on even one little baby step, so I want to throw out the stages so you can see where your mind and soul are and where they need to be in order to actually "do" something.

The TTM outlines five stages that reflect different time periods that we all deal with when thinking about making a meaningful change. They are:

Stage 1: Precontemplation

In this stage, you aren't even intending to take action in the foreseeable future (more than six months). I like to refer to this as the "intentionally clueless" stage, where maybe you've had so many starts and stops that you've essentially just given up and refuse to do any reading, talking, or thinking about your current shit show. Other characteristics of this stage include being resistant, unmotivated, and absolutely not ready, even if you get handed a golden opportunity on a silver platter. The good news is, because you bought this book and have invested your valuable time to read up to this point, you are definitely not in this stage. More than likely, you are now in Stage 2 or Stage 3.

Stage 2: Contemplation

Here is where things start happening. This stage is where you have the intention to change within the next six months. This is where you are aware of your current situation and know that making a change would be way better for you. In this stage, you are more aware of the benefits of making a change, but for some reason you're still coming up with a bunch of reasons why you shouldn't. If you did the split the paper trick and listed your pros for making the change on one side and the cons on the other, you'd come up with pretty close to an equal amount on both sides. This "selective ambivalence" means your Ego is still strong enough to keep you from creating enough mental leverage to justify the change.

This familiar "think and do nothing" stage is lovingly referred to as *procrastination*. Even though you can think of a thousand reasons to make a change, you still won't be able to make it happen. Even if you get pissed and have a "fuck it!" moment and start to move on something, you won't be able to follow through if you're in this stage because you won't have generated enough positive momentum or leverage to see yourself through the multiple hurdles or resistance. There's a chance you could be sitting in this stage with your wheels spinning in the mud. I like to refer to this as the stuck stage.

Stage 3: Preparation

This stage is where you've actually taken some preliminary steps, such as researching neighborhood gyms to join, looking up class schedules, or buying a self-help book, just to name a few examples. When in this stage, you are ready to rock to the point where measurable action will be taken within one month. You may actually even have a rough-sketch "plan of action" where you've broad-stroked some basic steps needed to climb out of your current muck.

At this point, you've overpowered that bastard Ego just enough to where you create some positive momentum, which typically takes on the form of obtaining knowledge about your next step so you can make a solid step right out of the gate. This is a good place to be because you have created an internal commitment to make the change. This is where you have actually started to see those "before" and "after" pictures in your head and you believe that the "after" is totally doable.

Stage 4: Action

As the name implies, this is where shit gets done. Technically, this step is when you make specific and measurable modifications in your life within the last six months, which means action(s) taken have changed your life enough to where you can tell you're in a different place physically, emotionally, or spiritually. This is the step that most people have accepted as the only behavioral change step, although you and I know it's only one of five stages. It's in this step where the process of experimenting, prototyping, and improvisation become solid game-changing tools. This is all about being in motion and doing whatever it takes to stay in motion. It goes without saying that this is where you're going to be confronted with the usual suspects known as fear, doubt, second-guessing, "failure," and possible self-sabotage.

However, because you already know those obstacles will jump in front of you and you now have the knowledge and tools to work through them, you'll be able to keep the ball rolling. And every time you successfully navigate one of those obstacles, it will make the next obstacle a little less daunting. Essentially, you are training yourself to be a superefficient life master by creating a flow of positive reinforcement as you consistently knock down those barriers that have been standing in front of you since you can remember.

Stage 5: Maintenance

This is the stage that begins at six months as your Stage 4 morphs into what I like to call a "tying your shoe" experience. What I mean is that all of that Jedi mind manipulation stuff you had to do on yourself to get you to take action begins to fade into the background as your new changes are now accepted as "the norm" and you don't have to think about them anymore. Like tying your shoes, you don't even have to think about how to cross and loop and tighten; it becomes automatic. The published theory indicates this stage lasts up to five years and is all about preventing relapse.

At this point, it's more about staying consistently aware of your new pattern so you can stay on top of any potential backsliding into the old pattern. It's really a double-edged sword because you want to be able to integrate a new pattern to a point where you don't have to think about it anymore, but you do have to consistently keep an eye on it, just to make sure there isn't any sign of a slide. This is most important when you are confronted by a significant emotional stressor, something that really jacks you up emotionally, like a bad breakup or a death, or even a bigtime positive thing like winning the lottery or getting a Venti when you paid for a Tall.

A significant emotional punch to the gut will weaken your system to the point where you have to do everything in your thinking power to steady yourself and remain on course while you simultaneously nurse your way through some serious emotional regrounding. This is the number-one reason for relapse, regardless of the behavior, because our emotional system is the most vulnerable to exterior forces. Good news is, you have the necessary heightened sense of awareness to be able to more quickly recover and get right back on the horse.

Since you are reading this right now, there's a good chance that you are either currently in Stage 2 (Contemplation) or Stage 3 (Preparation) or even Stage 4 (Action). That's a good sign because motivation to create change is like trying to roll a huge boulder down a hill. The first step of just getting the boulder to move from its fixed position at the top of the hill always takes the most energy. Since you're already on at least Stage 2 or 3, you've already jarred that boulder from its stationary position, creating some momentum and beginning its roll down the hill.

If in reading through these two stages you think you relate to being in the Contemplation Stage more than the Preparation Stage, then don't worry because the way I have the rest of the book set up, it will almost automatically move you from Contemplation into Preparation, leading to your first baby step into the world of Action. And if you resonate more with the Preparation Stage or, better yet, the Action Stage at this point, then you're ready to go.

 **VIDEO TIME: VIDEO #13**

CHAPTER 12

Smaller Is Better

"Love what you do. Get good at it. Competence
is a rare commodity in this day and age.
And let the chips fall where they may."

—JON STEWART

HOPEFULLY, YOU HAVE HAD SOME THOUGHTS go through your melon while you were reading about any number of little projects you can put together and complete. If you didn't think of anything, then I would highly suggest putting this book down, grabbing a pen and a piece of paper, and beginning to do some light brainstorming.

Remember, this is NOT supposed to be torture; it's supposed to be fun or at least mildly entertaining. It's supposed to be "doing" something that you *want* to do and that will result in something new when all is said and done. So, if you're feeling a massive level of resistance or have completely blocked your mind from thinking of even one stupid little action step, then you are completely on Ego-drive. And, if that's the case, then simply:

Get up, get a pen and a piece of paper, and start jotting down some cool things you would like to do. Seriously, the best way out of an Ego block is to "DO" something.

So, now let's say you have at least a couple of ideas about something to do. At this point, I would suggest your first project being the idea you believe can be easily accomplished within a relatively short period of time, while at the same time having enough "meaning" to it that you'll get a solid sense of satisfaction when it's completed.

Then, once you finish your first baby step (which I will help you plan out and see through to completion in the next chapter), you'll see that it actually will create a much more impactful ripple in your life than you would expect.

There's a very good chance that, even just after the first step, your life will shift to where your original list of "things I'd like to change" won't really apply. Basically, you'll have to reassess your life after every successful completion because your Foundation will grow ever stronger, and that may impact the big stuff on your list more than you think. It's just like those guys who demolish huge buildings. They don't pack the whole building to the brim with dynamite. Instead, they place the dynamite on a number of support beams throughout the building, which create a bunch of *small* explosions, which weaken the structure to where it collapses in on itself.

The more small steps you complete, the more you are weakening support for the big shit you want to change, which will ultimately lead to almost a chain reaction that will allow you to make a big shift in your own flow, which is the perfect scenario for making a big change. It's pretty fascinating how the tiniest of changes may produce big shifts in your life. The best part about that is, you'll have figured out that you didn't have to completely blow up your life in order to start molding it into the shape you want it to have.

Oh, by the way, in the process of doing this, you'll find your "endpoint," or where you envision your life going, will change as well. This is because what you think your Purpose and proper direction is right now may not be where you end up; your current self doesn't have all of the information and knowledge that you will eventually gain on your journey, and that newfound knowledge and experience may end up nudging you in a slightly different direction than what you originally thought. This is called "going with the flow."

It's Up to You to Make It Real

As important as the knowledge part is, and the ability to touch base with your True Self, and the ability to get centered and gain elevated awareness and presence, the most important step in this entire process is . . .

ACTION!

The entire point of putting the time and effort into improving yourself is to take action with strong purpose and an intention to live the most fulfilled life you can possibly live. So, keep moving, make mistakes, fall down, get up, brush yourself off, make adjustments, take appropriate actions, do it all over again, and again, and again. Think of the shitty stuff as road signs. The reason they pop up is because they have an urgent message for you. So, READ THEM, understand them, and make adjustments.

Think about it. If you weren't making progress, you wouldn't hit any of these hurdles. The fact you are coming up against barriers validates the fact that you are moving.

This is the *only* way to move forward. If you are not making any mistakes, you are not expanding. Stop fooling yourself because, in all seriousness, the world needs you. There aren't enough people who even know or believe that a fulfilled life is possible, let alone people who have strapped on a pair and jumped in, headfirst, like yourself.

There is a very powerful quotation from Teddy Roosevelt, the twenty-sixth president of the United States and the inspiration behind the teddy bear, which came from a speech titled "Citizenship in a Republic," which he delivered in Sorbonne, France, in 1910. The English is a little old school, but I think you'll get the point. Here it is:

> It is not the critic who counts; not the man who points out how the strong man stumbles, or where the doer of deeds could have done them better. The credit belongs to the man who is actually in the arena, whose face is marred by dust and sweat and blood; who strives valiantly; who errs, who comes short again and again, because there is no effort without error and shortcoming; but who does actually strive to do the deeds; who knows great enthusiasms, the great devotions; who spends himself in a worthy cause; who at the best knows in the end the triumph of high achievement, and who at the worst, if he fails, at least fails while daring greatly, so that his place shall never be with those cold and timid souls who neither know victory nor defeat.

Think about the successful people you admire, then ask yourself if they jumped into the ring and started swinging, or if they were one of the many who hung back and criticized like a little bitch. Now, it's YOUR TIME to strive, to err, and ultimately to SUCCEED!

 **VIDEO TIME: VIDEO #14**

CHAPTER 13

It's Now Time for Your Johnny Karate Super Awesome Project!

"You can't be that kid standing at the
top of the water slide overthinking it.
You have to go down the chute."

—TINA FEY

WE HAVE FINALLY REACHED THE PART OF THE SHOW where it's now your turn to think up, plan, and execute a small project. And, like I promised from the get-go, I am here to make this as easy and pain free as possible because I know how strangely difficult it is to actually get up off the book and step into the uncomfortable world of putting effort and thought into planning and executing something.

So, in the spirit of partnership, I am going to step-by-step this process right to your front door. I like to call this the "Johnny Karate Super Awesome Project" out of my unconditional love and admiration for *Parks and Recreation*, one of the five most brilliant comedy series ever televised.

Long story short, Johnny was a man-child and the star of a kids' TV show. Every show would consist of five parts:

1. Learn something new

2. Build something

3. Try something new

4. Karate chop something

5. Be nice to someone

For the record, and for the safety of those around you, let's say "Karate Chop Something" means to "chop" something out of your life that you know isn't doing you any favors.

So, for your Super Awesome project, I would like you to look at the stuff in your life that is a little out of whack and see if there is a pretty easy thing you can do on that list that fits under one of these five actions. I'm thinking something will, because these five things are pretty much the oversimplified foundation of any personal growth and development plan. Remember, the project has to "mean" something to you *and* benefit at least one other person in your life.

As you're thinking about that, let's take a look at how to set up a project.

A Less Boring Approach to Setting Up Your Project

Throughout the years, I've dealt with a lot of project management crap, and, to be honest, it's insanely boring. However, there is a widely accepted process of how to take a project step by step that is legit and easy to follow. So, I'll throw it out there for you so you can use it as a guide, not only for your Johnny Karate Super Awesome project, but for all your other future projects that may be slightly more involved (for those of you versed in business nomenclature, this is known as being "scalable").

For the purposes of us, right here and right now, I would like you to consider a project to be *"an idea that is carefully planned and designed to achieve a particular outcome."* And, with that in mind, here are the steps to develop your project.

Step 1 is conception. Ask yourself:

♦ What is my idea?

♦ Why do I want to do it?

♦ Who will it impact? (The answer should be at least your-self, plus one other.)

♦ When will it start and end? (ASAP, and within a week)

Step 1 is all about landing on an idea that will end up being a project that just nibbles at the edge of your cookie. This first baby-step project needs to be one you can start immediately and finish within a week. I'm sure you can think of something or someone you would like to:

♦ Learn more about

♦ Build or create

♦ Try for the first time

♦ Karate chop

♦ Be nice to

Make sure you can quickly and honestly answer the above what, why, who, and when. And, if you can and if it seems relatively easy and makes sense to you, then proceed to Step 2.

Step 2 is creating the plan.

For your first project, it should be a pretty basic plan with just a few steps. I suggest you write out the steps as a list or, in true Leslie Knope fashion, you can fill a binder with color-coded charts or Venn diagrams or create some fancy PowerPoint presentation. Whatever you decide, just make sure this one is simple and easy for you to follow and *complete.*

Step 3 is to execute the plan; make it happen.

By the time you get to this step, you should have already set the checkers on the board, and the next step is actually making the first move. This is the action part—taking the physical step into doing.

Step 4 is to make adjustments as needed.

Since this first baby-steps project is set up to be pretty simple, there probably won't be a lot of adjustments that have to be made, unless you totally screwed the pooch in the planning phase and find that you need to go back to that step and replan your attack. But if adjustments are needed, make them so your plan can move forward. That's the best part about starting off with a small project; you get to practice on small stuff, so if you do make mistakes, it's a lot easier to make an adjustment or two and get through it. And, in the process, you are actually learning how to effectively and efficiently complete a project.

Step 5 is when you close it up and feel the Bern!

Complete the project and allow yourself to feel good about completing the project. I'm not saying throw out your shoulder by giving overly aggressive high-fives to a million angels. I'm just saying feel solid and accomplished that you actually completed something you started because to the mind, it doesn't matter how big the project is. All the mind recognizes is you thought of something, planned something, took action on something, and made something happen. And, in the grand scheme of things, that's exactly what the entire point of our time together is about.

So, once you complete your first project and come down from your runner's high, it's time to take a couple steps back and look at what you've just created and what kind of a change ripple it may have sent through your life.

Initially, there's a chance it may not look like it did a whole lot, and maybe it didn't move any mountains, but that wasn't the point of the first project anyway. The point of this first baby-step Johnny Karate Super Awesome Project was to prove to yourself that you could do it and, at the same time, to begin to reprogram your brain to being more open to expansion and change.

So, that's the step-by-step of the project, laid out for you like a picnic blanket under the big oak tree at the church clam bake. In the next chapter, I'll illustrate some actual project examples that follow this step-by-step format and fall under one of the five Johnny Karate categories.

 VIDEO TIME: VIDEO #15

Actual Super Awesome Project Examples

"'Why the fuck not me?' should be your motto."

—MINDY KALING

EVEN THOUGH I THINK I'VE LAID THIS OUT in a way that's pretty easy to follow, I know there's a chance you may be mentally blocking yourself from thinking about how your project would look in real time, especially if you are just emerging from the Contemplation Stage or a relatively new resident of the Preparation Stage. So, I'm going to give you an example of how a small project is thought up, planned, and executed, using the five Johnny Karate things you can do. The way I've designed this process, it will allow you to trick your Ego into thinking you're just completing a task or doing something fun.

When you read through these examples you may think they are so easy or basic that they shouldn't even "count" toward your personal growth process. But the deceptively easy aspect of this process is the secret sauce to success because it was created to unstick you from a stage of change that, up until now, has not allowed you to do something that aligns with your overall life meaning and Purpose.

Learn Something New (Example)

1. Conception: Ask Yourself . . .

◆ *What is my idea?* To learn enough Spanish to thank Manny for being such an awesome coworker.

◆ *Why do I want to do it?* Because I want to show him a level of respect by learning a little bit of his language and acknowledging his amazing work ethic. That dude shows up every day on time and works his ass off and never says boo about anything.

◆ *Who will it impact?* My coworker and me.

◆ *When will it start and end?* Three days: one day to figure out how to translate a phrase, one day to practice, and one day to deliver the message.

2. The Plan

◆ *Step 1:* On Day 1, for a couple of hours after I get home from work, I'll go online and find out how to say in Spanish, "Hey, Manny, I really appreciate your hard work, day in and day out! Thanks, man."

◆ *Step 2:* On Day 2, I will spend a couple of hours after work memorizing the phrase.

◆ *Step 3:* On Day 3, I'll say the phrase to Manny when he's done with his shift.

3. Execute—Make It Happen

◆ I looked up the phrase (thanks, AltaVista), took to memorizing it the second night, and said it to Manny at the end of his shift on the third night.

4. Make Adjustments as Needed

◆ When I was saying it to Manny, I fucked up the word for "appreciate," so I had to take a quick pause and grab the written version from my pocket so I could get it right, then I finished what I had to say.

5. Close It Up and Feel the Bern!

◆ As I finished, Manny had an "I can't believe he actually spoke Spanish" look on his face and then cracked a grateful grin and told me, "*Mucho apreciar.*"

Build Something (Example)

1. Conception: Ask Yourself . . .

◆ *What is my idea?* Instead of doing the usual, I'm going to build or create a birthday card to give to my smokin' hot significant other.

◆ *Why do I want to do it?* Because I want to show her how much she means to me and I know that, since I put the time and effort into creating it myself, it will be extra special to her because I don't show her often enough how much I appreciate her love and support in my life. As a side note, I also know it will lead to mind-blowing sex—not that that is my objective, but I'm certainly okay with it being a healthy byproduct of my project.

◆ *Who will it impact?* My girl, me, and our relationship.

◆ *When will it start and end?* Two days, ending on her birthday.

2. The Plan

- *Step 1:* First day, stop by the store after work and pick up some heavier cardstock paper, some glue, macaroni, glitter, stickers, and an 8-pack of lead-based crayons (I'm going full on kindergarten).

- *Step 2:* Then, day 2 (her birthday), I'll have about an hour before she gets home to put it together.

3. Execute—Make It Happen

- I stopped by the store, picked up the card-building materials, and made sure I put them in my trunk so she wouldn't see them lying around the house.

- On her birthday, I thought a little about what I wanted to do in terms of a design and when I got home, I put it together. (I look forward to finding glitter around the house for the next several months.)

4. Make Adjustments as Needed

- I actually had to start over (Note: Buy more than one piece of cardstock paper, just in case) because I messed up the "B" in Birthday (looked like the chicken who wrote it had a stroke on the paper), and I had a slight issue with the glitter being uncooperative in properly and efficiently sticking to the Elmer's Glue. Oh, and make sure you wait until it's completely dry before attempting to close the card. Barely averted a disaster there.

5. Close It Up and Feel the Bern!

- I wanted to make sure the timing was just right, so I waited until right after dinner. Then, as we comfortably sat on the couch with a red cup full of Franzia Reserve, I brought out her gift bag and pulled the card out, handing it to her first. And, as expected, she loved it. I don't even think she really cared about the professionally bedazzled iPhone case I got her for a present. My project was a success!

Try Something New (Example)

1. Conception: Ask Yourself . . .

◆ *What is my idea?* I am going to go up to three people I don't know at a party and initiate a conversation.

◆ *Why do I want to do it?* Because I usually don't put myself out there and start up conversations.

◆ *Who will it impact?* Me. It will help me to get over a fear of starting a conversation with people I don't know. And it will also impact the three people I talk to because I'm going to make sure I bring good energy and sneak in at least one compliment to each of them.

◆ *When will it start and end?* Beginning about an hour before the party and ending when I leave the party.

2. The Plan

◆ *Step 1:* Before the party, I'm going to go over the steps of a basic conversation plan, which happen to be: Make an observation about what someone is doing or wearing or talking about (as you strategically eavesdrop), then approach them with a form of "Hi" and launch into your observation, then immediately follow with a question about the observation, like, "Hey, that's a honey of an ankle bracelet! Is it supposed to be that big or did it slide down there?"

- *Step 2:* Get to the party, have one drink (just to have in my hand; don't get hammered before doing this).

- *Step 3:* Take a quick look around the party. Notice something about someone that I can start a conversation about, make an observation, and do the approach. Then throw out the observation comment and follow with the question and see where it goes. For the purposes of this project, I'm going to keep the conversation short and just follow with one additional question unless they launch into a full-blown rant. If that occurs, I'll put about five minutes into it before ejecting.

3. Execute—Make It Happen

- As I was getting ready for the party, I went over the steps and promised myself three things: I will follow through on this because it's a gift to those I speak to. I won't use this technique to hit on girls because that's not what this project is about (although this conversation technique works great for breaking the ice). I will wait until I've talked to three people before initiating my binge drinking.

- Arrived at the party, grabbed a drink. Some guy was standing next to the booze table with a tattoo of what appeared to be a baby snowy owl in asymmetrical overalls flipping me off with his right wing (appeared to be his middle feather). Of course, that lead to my first interaction-observation-question session of the night. I'll leave the story behind the ink for another time. Then, it was on to my next victim. With the momentum from the first dude, I actually had my three interactions one after the other, which left me plenty of time to booze it up. Thank God for Lyft, right?!

4. Make Adjustments as Needed

◆ The second interaction I had was with a girl where I observed that she came to the party in a sweet pair of Daisy Dukes, so my observation to her was, "Wow, Daisy Dukes, nice! What compelled you to rock those tonight?" Well, as complimentary as I thought I sounded, she actually thought I was making fun of her and she gave me *that* glare. So, I quickly rephrased my observation to, "I'm just sayin' I'm a huge fan of the style and of anyone who keeps that flame alive . . . I love it." And, since I restated myself by smiling through my delivery, she picked up that I was being sincere and eased up. We actually had a nice conversation after that about her wanting to hit on some dude she already met at the party because they had matching tattoos.

5. Close It Up and Feel the Bern!

◆ That night, seated in the corner booth at Drunk Denny's with a couple of my friends (I think), I had a chance to reflect back and feel the Bern of satisfaction that "I did it," and I know that I gave the gift of a nice conversation with all three of the people I chose to approach. Now I have to decide between the Rooty Tooty Fresh and Fruity or Moons Over My Hammy.

Karate Chop Something (Example)

1. Conception: Ask Yourself . . .

◆ *What is my idea?* To "cut down" on the amount of time I'm on social media.

◆ *Why do I want to do it?* Because I feel like it burns time and keeps me from focusing on taking action in my own life to create my own cool experiences and deeper relationships with my circle of close friends.

◆ *Who will it impact?* Me and my close friends and family whom I will have more time for once I get my face out of my phone.

◆ *When will it start and end?* It will start immediately, and I'll give it a full week to sink in and hopefully I will start to form a new habit of reduced use.

2. The Plan

◆ *Step 1:* Instead of checking my phone right as I get up in the morning, I will do my get-ready routine, eat my breakfast, get to work, go through work email, then give myself fifteen minutes to check social media.

◆ *Step 2:* I will not stick my nose in my phone until lunch, where I'll give myself fifteen minutes to check, unless I'm having lunch with someone. If I am, then I will keep my phone out of sight and have a nice, interactive lunch, person-to-person style, without any distractions.

◆ *Step 3:* I will then give myself fifteen minutes either right after work or before I go to bed, and I'll make sure I put the phone on silent so I don't get woken up by some random text from a Nigerian prince looking for someone to take a couple million dollars off his hands.

- *Step 4:* I will set aside a chunk of my new free time to call a friend or call my mom, or research something I would like to do or would at least like to know more about, or use that open time to grab a book, or just have a peaceful moment to myself, and/or maybe do some pants-optional bongo playing.

3. Execute—Make It Happen

- I put a sticky note on my phone so I would remember not to check it, and because it's such a habit, it was admittedly hard not to check.

- I kept my phone in my pocket during lunch with a couple of coworker buddies, even though they had theirs out, checking them every few minutes. It was weird watching that happen and realizing, *Damn, is that what I look like?*

- I fought off the urge to keep the phone on in case of a random 2 a.m. drunk booty call, and I turned it off and actually moved the charger out to the kitchen so when I woke up it wouldn't be taunting me.

- I made it a point to talk to someone different every day of the week, which actually led to planning an impromptu little get-together at my place on Saturday. And I found the bottomless bongo playing to be an effective tool at minimizing my neighbor's passing glances into my front window as he drags his overtly lazy Cocker-Labra-Chihuahua-Doodle over to what appears to be the chosen canine bowel dumping spot, which is conveniently located in front of *my* house.

4. Make Adjustments as Needed

◆ I knew I was going to have an early, pointless meeting at work, so I shifted my morning social media time to right after breakfast and before I jumped into the car to head to work.

5. Close It Up and Feel the Bern!

◆ After looking back on the week, I could see that it opened up some good quality time, and I was able to have some great conversations with friends and also was able to make a solid dent in the newest Nicholas Sparxxx novel, *Massaging My Bottle* (he just gets me).

Be Nice to Someone (Example)

1. Conception: Ask Yourself . . .

◆ *What is my idea?* To be nice to someone that I feel may need it.

◆ *Why do I want to do it?* Because it makes me feel good that I'm cheering someone up and that I'm creating a ripple effect that may result in his turning around and being nice to someone else—paying it forward.

◆ *Who will it impact?* Me, the person I'm nice to, and maybe even more people down the line.

◆ *When will it start and end?* I'll give myself a full day to take a look around and see where I can use my super-power for good.

2. The Plan

◆ *Step 1:* Remind myself at the beginning of the day to

be extra aware of people around me so I can spot an opportunity where someone needs some of my "nice."

- *Step 2:* Spot someone in need of my services and immediately help or offer to help.

- *Step 3:* If they do happen to say, "Thank you," then respond with an appropriate, "You're welcome," "No problem," "No worries," "My pleasure," etc.

3. Execute—Make It Happen

- I was strolling down the condiment aisle at the store when I saw this cute little older lady trying to reach for some organic mustard on the top shelf. She clearly had no chance of grabbing it, so I hustled over there and asked if I could get that for her. She said something like, "Oh my goodness gracious! Yes, that would be lovely." So, I grabbed the jar and handed it to her, and she said, "Thank you very much, young man," and I said, "You are very welcome." Then, after a brief moment of hesitation, she asked me what I thought about open marriages and wrinkles (in that order). So I sloppily faked an Eastern European accent, said something like, "Me know not English much very," and hastily abandoned my cart, mid-aisle, immediately initiating full Tom Cruise sprint mode in pursuit of the quickest exit possible and the safe haven of my own vehicle. I have yet to return to that market or regain my taste for organic mustard.

4. Make Adjustments as Needed

- I consider my hasty retreat from the octogenarian swinger to be a valid adjustment.

5. Close it Up and Feel the Bern!

♦ I felt good about keeping myself aware enough to spot the little old lady's dilemma and was glad I could be of service. I knew that she felt grateful and that felt good to me. Not only did I get a chance to help someone, but got propositioned in the process. And, in hindsight, I have no problem with that.

It's All About the Small Rocks

> "The man who moves a mountain
> begins by carrying away small stones."
>
> —CONFUCIUS

You can see that all of the examples I gave you were relatively simple projects in terms of planning and complexity. I mean, it shouldn't take some complicated plan to go out and be nice to someone. But remember the purpose of this exercise is not to *just* complete some project. It's to take a good look at the parts of your life that you would like to gently nudge in a different direction, and then plan a simple first project to start the ball rolling in the right direction.

Like I said at the beginning of this, the first project is *supposed* to be almost too easy because the first step is *not* about moving mountains; it's about picking up some small rocks and throwing them in the direction you want. Basically, it's about subtly reprogramming your mind to understand the process of taking an idea and putting it into action. And when the project is small and simple, your Ego will think it's too small to give any attention to, and you'll be able to sneak around the Ego and begin to reprogram yourself so you are able to conceptualize, plan, and complete projects on a consistent basis. The more you use these steps and the more projects you complete, the more confident you will become in being able to steer your life in any direction you choose without the Ego getting in the way and messing with your mind.

Once you complete your first project, I highly suggest writing down some notes about what worked and what didn't and how, maybe, your thinking or actions changed in the course of completing the project. I mean, you just went through an experiment for the sole purpose of learning more about yourself, so jot down some stuff so you can use it later.

After a quick recap on your success, I would suggest taking a quick breather before starting the thinking process about your next project. With the positive momentum from your first success, you should feel compelled to get your next one going within a day or two. Do you see how this could potentially snowball into some serious movement in your life? And it all began with some overly simple act.

Like I said a while ago, don't overthink the room on this stuff; it's pretty basic once you learn the steps.

 **VIDEO TIME: VIDEO #16**

CHAPTER 15

In a Nutshell

> "I believe that if life gives you lemons, you should make lemonade . . . and try to find somebody whose life has given them vodka, and have a party."
> —RON WHITE

SO, NOW WHAT? BY THIS TIME, you should be pretty overwhelmed because this program covers a lot of stuff. And although it provides a good working framework to operate from, True Self understanding and fulfillment do not magically appear after you get schooled on the concepts and the tools/techniques to get you there. That would be like a carpenter expecting a house to already be built just because he's got a fresh set of plans in his hand and his new tools just got delivered. He still has to read the plans and use the tools to build the damn thing, and so do you.

When consulting with clients, I constantly remind them that living a fulfilled life is a marathon, not a sprint. This program was developed so you can create your own marathon course to get you to where you want to go.

One More Recap for the Road

From start to finish, True Self training involves:

1. Understanding the basic components of life, like Unity, Big World, Inner World, True Self, Ego, Foundation, Vision, Purpose, and Gift

2. Discovering where you are in your life, right now, through answering a few questions and looking at your answers from a number of different perspectives

3. Painting a picture of what your life could look like if you made some adjustments

4. Comparing where you are right now with how your life could be

5. Using tools and techniques to bring you more in alignment with how cool your life could really be

6. And, finally, taking ACTION—thinking, planning, and completing a project based on your newfound knowledge and awareness

You know, I always thought it was a little patronizing when I would read through a self-improvement book and the author would drop the whole, "Just the fact that you are reading this right now means you're way ahead of the game." However, in creating this program and working with clients who have taken the time and put some blood, sweat, and tears into this material, I completely agree with that notion.

I know I've said this a couple of times already, and I'm

not trying to validate your worth with some hokey compliment, but **you are way ahead of the curve.**

Whether you follow every step of this program, or just certain pieces that work for you, or you believe it doesn't fit you but you will continue to search for something that does, I want you to know that you have my mad respect! I wish you nothing less than a completely fulfilled life!

"The journey of a thousand miles
begins with a single step."

—LAO TZU

 **VIDEO TIME: VIDEO #17**

Resources

Throughout our journey together, I've referenced a lot of books and shows and movies and whatnot that have had a huge impact on me. And, I'm thinking, if you got something out of this book, there's a good chance you have a similar take on the world as I do, and you might get some big-time benefits from the stuff that influenced me along my path of discovery. So, here you go.

Stuff to Read

The Power of Now: A Guide to Spiritual Enlightenment by Eckhart Tolle

I reread this book almost once a month. (I have highlighted sections over the years, so I can get through a reread in less than 45 minutes.) I have to say, for grounding purposes and getting you to focus awareness on the Now, this book is my favorite. Eckhart Tolle was just this guy who hit rock bottom and had a nervous breakdown on a park bench, all of a sudden coming into the realization that life was much more than the stuff going on around him. This guy was blessed with the ability to boil very complex concepts down to easily understood life guidelines that anyone can immediately start to implement into their life. You can find used copies of this book on Amazon for a couple of bucks and, in all seriousness, it will be the best investment you can make for yourself.

You Are a Badass: How to Stop Doubting Your Greatness and Start Living an Awesome Life by Jen Sincero

I can't tell you how fired up I was to see this book on the bestseller list. If you have already taken a look at Jen's book, you can probably tell we have a very similar approach to this stuff. Jen writes with such honesty and rawness that reading the book feels like you're talking with a few of your buddies at a kegger. I think she does an amazing job at explaining the forces around you and the fact that you are your own worst enemy in most situations. She is unapologetic, funny as hell, and is not afraid to throw a "fuck" around now and again. She has fantastic stories and the book is very inspiring. Thanks, Jen, and I look forward to reading more of your stuff.

Man's Search for Meaning by Viktor E. Frankl

Viktor was a psychiatrist who was imprisoned in a Nazi death camp during World War II. During those insanely horrific years in the camp, he was able to develop a whole new theory of psychotherapy called logotherapy. *Logo* means "meaning," and his approach is based on the belief that a human's primary motivational force is his or her search for meaning. During my grad school days, I did a lot of reading up on logotherapy and Frankl, and I have to say, it really speaks to me. As you can tell, the whole meaning thing is a cornerstone in my philosophy and writings as well.

Man's Search for Meaning is divided into two distinct sections. The first is the story of Frankl's time in the camp, and it's freaking unbelievable what that guy went through and witnessed. This part of the book is a real eye-opener to how evil people can get and how inspirational some other people can be through the worst of times. The second section of the book is about his logotherapy. Frankl does a great job at walking the reader through the concepts and his philosophy of life that have had an amazing influence on both philosophy and psychology theories over the past sixty-plus years. It's all about giving your life meaning and how to go about finding meaning and using it as a guide to living a fulfilled life.

The Fifth Discipline: The Art & Practice of the Learning Organization by Peter Senge

Peter Senge is well-known in the corporate world. His expertise is in building organizations and management consulting. Written with a bit of a business slant, the overall structure development of his concepts is brilliant. Basically, Senge outlines five disciplines you and I need to instill in ourselves to run a successful life, and the disciplines, or concepts, are based in science, psychology, philosophy, and spirituality. Personally, I got a ton out of reading this book, especially regarding the "U" process, which is a way to look at the process of becoming aware enough, then to learn, then to do. Sound familiar? It's all about systems thinking and seeing all the little bits of life as a part of a grand system, and then how to see patterns within the system. And, being a business-oriented book, you would assume it is pretty dry, but it's not; it's a kick-ass read.

The Celestine Prophecy: An Adventure by James Redfield

I can say, without a shred of doubt, that this is the book that changed my life the most. I first read this book back when it came out, about twenty or so years ago. It was during a time when I was floundering, without an idea of who I was or what I wanted to do with my life. Then, I somehow heard about The Celestine Prophecy and decided to pick it up. The cool part about this book is that it is written as an Indiana Jones type of adventure/thriller. It literally starts out with the author being chased by people, and he doesn't know why. I dig books that draw you in right away.

The overall premise of the story is about the discovery of an ancient manuscript in the jungles of Peru that include nine insights into life and the full manifestation of human beings into a pure energy state. Yeah, that may sound a little tinfoil-on-the-head, but stay with me. The story is set up so that the author goes on this journey to find one insight at a time, with all of the insights building upon each other until the final piece of the puzzle comes to light. The insights are based on ancient South American and Eastern philosophical concepts, and the book is essentially a guidebook that takes the reader on a journey of self-discovery and introspection. Like I said at the outset, this book completely changed my life; it set me on the path to where I am today. Side note: The book was made into a movie. Read the book instead.

Poke the Box: When Was the Last Time You Did Something for the First Time? by Seth Godin

For the record, I am a huge Seth Godin fan. Seth is a business marketing guy with a background in computer science and marketing. By now, he's written probably close to twenty books. I'm just listing this one, but I've read five or six, and they're all brilliant. This is another business-oriented book that applies to overall life concepts, similar to *The Fifth Discipline*. In *Poke the Box*, Seth points the finger at the terrible way some of our institutions are set up and how we sleepwalk through a lot of stuff that we shouldn't put up with. This book gets the reader to think about his or her personal value and uniqueness and how nothing happens unless you instigate, question, "poke the box," and learn from your nonconformity. It's all about creating your own road map; stop following and begin to dive into yourself and the unique contribution you have to give. This book is a super quick read (eighty pages), but is packed with some amazing insights and guidelines that you can use every day to center yourself and consistently operate from your unique True Self.

Bossypants by Tina Fey

I'm going to come right out and admit it: **I'm in love with Tina Fey.** She is funny as hell, brilliant, quick-witted, and super easy on the eyes. This woman has faced some serious stuff in her time and continues to have the awareness and optimism to shape those experiences into some seriously funny shit. This book isn't necessarily a philosophical read or full of spiritual insights, but it does tell Tina's story of growing up and facing hardships and how she navigated the crap and became successful. Plus, there's a lot of behind-the-scenes talk about *30 Rock* and *SNL*, two of my favorite shows of all time. It's a really funny and inspiring read.

How to Win Friends & Influence People by Dale Carnegie

This book falls under the category of "No, duh! Of course I'm going to mention this one." An absolute classic, I'm thinking you've already dove into this one. If not, it should be on your "must-read" list. Although first published in 1937, it is still considered one of the best people-skills books ever written. Carnegie's message is that success is primarily based on your ability to express your ideas, to assume leadership, and to get people excited about your idea. He goes through some skills to relate to people in a genuine and caring way, so they don't feel manipulated, how to get people interested in your idea, and how to change minds without creating resentment. It includes the six ways to make people like you and the twelve ways to win people over to your way of thinking. Personally, I love the whole book, especially Chapter 6 when Carnegie talks about how to handle complaints by letting people unload while staying unreactive, then ask them questions to bring them back around to a place where you can have a constructive dialogue with them to solve the problem.

The Artist's Way: A Spiritual Path to Higher Creativity
by Julia Cameron

This is the book that talks about how important and effective journaling is as a tool for focus and uncovering hidden programs. I think Julia Cameron does an outstanding job at walking the reader through certain reasons why our creative process gets blocked from time to time, and she offers up a really good plan of action to get you unstuck and back on the road to creation. She wrote the book to appeal to artists who have come up against a writing block or general creative block, but I think the concepts and exercises apply to anyone who is confused or directionless. She does a masterful job at providing tools for grounding and helping anyone to open up their imagination, and that is something we could all use.

Media Stuff

Big Think (*BigThink.com*)

I actually follow Big Think on Facebook, but you can also go to the website. I click on this page's articles at least once a day, and way more than any other page on Facebook. It is full of thoughtful, unbiased (I think so, anyway) articles and videos on a wide variety of issues including philosophy, psychology, self-improvement, science, politics, community awareness, current topical stuff—just about anything you can imagine. The best part about the articles here is that they are really great at keeping up with the stuff that is important for us as individuals and for the world community as a whole. Plus, they do an amazing job at bringing in the top experts in a wide variety of fields to do relatively short video opinions about important topics. I guarantee you will feel smarter and more informed the more you click on this page.

Facebook (*Facebook.com*)

Truth be told, I am a relative newcomer to Facebook. I think I started about three or four years ago, and only after being hassled by most of the people in my inner circle to do so. I did not initially drink the social media Kool-Aid, and being a Gen Xer, I think I had some generational snobbery going on, thinking that this whole social media stuff is just a waste of time. (I actually called it "The Facebook" for a while, just to piss people off.) However, after jumping in and witnessing the unequaled power of Facebook to connect and communicate, I was sold.

My rationale at the beginning was to use it more for my Java Bud stuff, so I set up a page and started posting my podcasts and videos and shares of great articles I found while scrolling. This led me to my epiphany that, like anything, this powerful tool can be really great or really shitty. And, what I really dig is that there are so many insanely amazing content creators out there, Big Think being one of my favorites. These sites have provided me so much worthwhile information that I know I probably never would have found doing old-school-style research. As a content provider myself, this site has the most brilliant marketing platform in that you can basically pinpoint any type of niche market you want (yeah, it's pay to play, but everything has a cost and this is well worth the investment for me). So, as much as some people like to bag on Facebook, I think the site is amazing and, in digging into the company culture a little, I think the organization is a terrific model of how a company should be structured and operated in this current time period and for years to come; the level of built-in flexibility and adaptation and fluidity is really impressive. I didn't want to slobber all over Facebook, but I needed to go on the record to show my appreciation of how it's positively impacted my life. Thanks, Mark!

NPR (*NPR.org*)

For transparency's sake, my politics are pretty moderate. I'm "that guy" who says I'm a fiscal conservative and a social liberal, which basically means I'm purple. That being said, I think NPR does a great job at delivering the news and really good articles on breakthroughs in science, great pieces on art and culture, and an article or video on current topic stuff from time to time. This is another one of the pages I liked on Facebook. I also listen to NPR in the morning and a lot of times in the car when I feel I want to be connected to important stuff going on.

30 Rock (*NBC, currently on Netflix and Hulu*)

Outside of my previous pledge of undying love and devotion to Tina Fey, I am a *huge* fan of this show. *30 Rock* is not just any sitcom. It's so smartly written that I have to pay attention so I don't miss anything. This is the perfect show for me because it challenges me and my depth of humor to find the joke and, more important, to get the joke. I love how deceptive it can be, taking on typical sitcom themes and at the same time making huge and impactful observations on so many of our fucked up human archetypes. I respect the hell out of this show because it respects its audience and, with the exception of Season 1 (they were finding their voice during this whole season), the series delivers top-shelf quality entertainment in every single show. There is no sense of taking a week off with this show, and I really appreciate that. I included this show in this resource section because I think it does a tremendous job at exposing a lot of the bullshit we deal with on a daily basis and provides great examples of dealing with surrounding idiots.

Parks and Recreation (*NBC, currently on Netflix and Hulu*)

In getting hooked on this show, I discovered something very significant about my particular sense of humor—it's the characters' "reactions" to idiotic things that are the funniest to me. You also see a lot of this in *The Office*, but I think Amy Poehler and the rest of the cast do a masterful job at summing up just how ridiculous life can be. The show is played pretty straight, like a camera crew following around a bunch of public servants. However, every character is so distinct and reflects such a unique personality archetype that it makes the interaction between the cast members a poetic swirl of contrasting perspectives and world-views, so you find yourself with the ability to actually relate to each personality in their own weird way. This goes right along with the section in the book where I talked about being able to understand that each person lives in their own unique world inside their own head, and it's our job to understand that and accept that before we attempt to communicate with them. It's also sweet and very genuine in its approach. Just like *30 Rock,* the first season and about half of the second season are just okay. This show finds its legs after that and is absolutely fucking brilliant.

The Matrix (*Warner Bros. Pictures*)

This movie is very important to me for what it represents. The deeply impactful underlying meaning of this movie is that most of us are caught in our Ego world, more or less slaves of a system that we didn't choose and that doesn't serve our best interest to find our True Self, and live on that level of awareness and understanding. I mean, this movie spells out exactly what's going on with society and also shows there is an opportunity to choose the right pill and open yourself up to a level of awareness where you can literally see the patterns in the world and then be in a position to make a very aware, conscious choice at any moment. It basically puts this book in movie form. Now, I know for some of you, you may not be able to get past the Rock 'Em Sock 'Em Robots stuff, but the underlying message is one of profound meaning and power: Once you take the leap to find out more, be open to the knowledge, be okay with getting beat up and falling off tall buildings and failing during your discovery process, then you will find yourself in a place where "you just know." Like Morpheus says to Neo during the Kung Fu fight, "Stop trying to hit me, and hit me!" No, I don't believe we are being used as living batteries by the machines. But I do believe that most people live reactive and mostly unconscious lives unless they get that burr up their ass that there's something more and then go about honing their self-awareness and clarity of Purpose—just like you are doing right now.

Learning Stuff

Synergenics (*Ness Carroll*)

Along with the brilliant Phyllis Nordstrom, I studied with Ness as a part of my Ph.D. program at the International University. Along with her groundbreaking doctorate work, Ness has developed a personal growth and development company known as Synergenics. I give Ness most of the credit for opening up my mind to a more holistic view of life and world and purpose. I initially chose the Ph.D. program at International because it offered so much more depth of understanding and deep philosophical concepts, which I believe are way more impactful in empowering a person to discover and create than the standard "therapy" option that is mostly focused on symptoms and bringing patients in for a long-term money grab. Yeah, I know, some therapy is very helpful (hell, I mentioned it in the book), but not in a lot of cases where you need more knowledge, structure, and motivation to transition into a higher frequency level of your life. That is what I do, and that is the education you will receive from Ness in her Synergenics program. She calls it a Methodology for Transcendence.

Along with the one-on-one work, Ness also works with groups and companies and also does a lot of channeling work and mystical healing stuff. This is where she goes a little further than I do, but those of you who are into that, she's a master. In addition to Synergenics, she has a blog at www.spiritsblog.com and educational CDs at www.lifelove andlaughter.com. I highly recommend you check out her stuff.

Acknowledgments

Yes, I realize that pretty much the only people reading this section are the people that "expect" to be listed. So, the people that I do list think, *Hey, there I am, as expected.* Or even better, they could pull the Italian mother card with, *There I am! It's a good thing—wait a minute, why am I not listed first?* Then, there are the ones who expect to and don't get mentioned. There's no way to spin it: This section is basically a shit sandwich.

Nevertheless, there are some very special people who have supported me throughout the years and helped me to persevere to create and share this message with you: Rachel, Josh, Eve, Melanie, Chris, Ashley, two Mariahs, another Chris, Phyllis, Ness, Lexi, Melissa, and Nicole, along with the good men and women who helped me design and print this thing. I am certainly not surrounded by idiots when I refer to this group (well, most of the time). Thank you, all!

About the Author

Tony Dufresne is a millennial mentor, leadership-transformation-success coach, life strategist, writer, speaker, single dad, winner of multiple all-you-can-drink Ovaltine contests, and a thousandaire entrepreneur who considers coffee to be its own food group. The fancily written documents on his wall include a PhD in applied philosophy, a master's in psychology, and a personal trainer certification with specialization in behavioral change through the National Association of Sports Medicine (NASM). Tony is also a trained facilitator, a member of the Psi Chi (the International Honor Society in Psychology), and ardent collector of vintage Ukrainian pornography.

After fifteen years of study and research, Tony created the Surrounded by Idiots Radio Podcast and Java Bud, an online coaching and resource site that has helped countless human beings (and one enthusiastic feral cat) to get really clear on what they want their life to be about with the tools to make it happen. A self-proclaimed nonconformist, Tony never wanted to fit into the mold of a traditional therapist or life coach, which is reflected in his non-sugarcoated, direct, snarky, and dry-witted approach to educating and motivating his clients to make their own unique mark on this world.

Okay, I'm being told my time is up, so you can read and hear more by going to Javabud.com. Stay thirsty, my friends.

Ten percent of the net proceeds from the sale of this book will be donated to Singleton Moms, a nonprofit organization based in Scottsdale, Arizona, that provides resources to single parents and children going through cancer treatment. I served on the Singleton Moms board of directors for four years and have seen the incredible impact this group, specifically the organization's founder Jody Farley, has had on hundreds of families that are battling this terrible disease. If you would like more information about Singleton Moms, visit www.singletonmoms.org.

If you don't have a regular nonprofit that you support, I highly encourage you to reach out. Hell, this whole book has been about helping you to help yourself to help others, so it would only make sense, right?

Made in the USA
San Bernardino, CA
15 January 2018